CHRONOLOGICAL
ASPECTS
OF THE
LIFE OF CHRIST

CHRONOLOGICAL
ASPECTS
OF THE
LIFE OF CHRIST

HAROLD W. HOEHNER

Academie
Books Grand Rapids,
Michigan
Zondervan Publishing House

CHRONOLOGICAL ASPECTS OF THE LIFE OF CHRIST
© 1977 by The Zondervan Corporation
© 1973, 1974, 1975 by Dallas Theological Seminary

Requests for information should be addressed to:
Zondervan Publishing House
Academic and Professional Books
Grand Rapids, Michigan 49530

Library of Congress Cataloging in Publication Data

Hoehner, Harold W.
    Chronological aspects of the life of Christ.
    Bibliography.
    Includes index.
    1. Jesus Christ—Chronology. I. Title.
BT303.H58   232.9'01   76-30350

ISBN 0-310-26211-9

Printed in the United States of America

HB 04.04.2024

To Mrs. Edna Welch and her late
husband Arthur who introduced
me not only to the life of Christ
but also to life in Christ

Contents

Illustrations

Preface

Jesus Christ entered into the history of our world. Christianity, therefore, has historical basis. The backbone of history is chronology. Whereas history is a systematic account of events in relation to a nation, institution, science, or art; chronology is a science of time. It seeks to establish and arrange the dates of past events in their proper sequence. Thus chronology serves as necessary framework upon which the events of history may be fitted.

This is not a book on the life of Christ but it attempts to establish certain fixed dates of our Lord's life. It is hoped that this work will serve as a framework for the life of Christ. Many times there is a vagueness of dates in the life of Christ. The reason for this is twofold. First, there is not a series of concrete dates given in the Gospels. More important to the Gospel writers (as well as other writers of that day) was to record the facts of the events and words of their master than to record the time they happened. Second, since there are great differences of opinion among scholars concerning each of these events given in this book there is a tendency to abandon the effort rather than attempt to see if one can make sense with the date of each event as well as seeing if they can make a sensible chronological scheme from all the events.

However, if one is convinced of a grammatical-historical interpretation of the New Testament, one should attempt to deal with the chronological notes in the Gospels in order to give one a proper historical perspective to the life of Christ.

This book was first presented as a series of articles in *Bibliotheca Sacra*. A word of appreciation is due the editors of *Bibliotheca Sacra* for granting me permission to reproduce the articles and charts in a revised form. Also, I want to express my appreciation to Cambridge University Press for granting me permission to reproduce portions from my book *Herod Antipas* for a greater part of chapter II in this book.

I want to especially thank Mr. James C. Killion who read every stage of this work several times and who made many valuable suggestions.

Chapter I

The Date of Christ's Birth

In Luke 2:10-11 the angel of the Lord announced to the shepherds in the fields, "Do not be afraid for I bring you good news of great joy which shall be for all people that today a Savior, who is Christ the Lord, was born in the city of David. And this will be a sign to you: you will find a baby wrapped in cloths and lying in a manger." The announcement is familiar to all Christians. The Bible portrays that the eternal Christ became incarnate beginning with His birth in Bethlehem of Judah. It is therefore fitting to begin this study of the chronology of the life of Christ at His birth.

THE YEAR OF CHRIST'S BIRTH

The earliest Christians were not as much concerned about the date as the fact of the birth of Christ. Chronological notes, such as "In the fifteenth year of the reign of Tiberius" (Luke 3:1) marking the commencement of John the Baptist's ministry, were sufficient.

In A.D. 525 Pope John I asked Dionysius, a Scythian monk, to prepare a standard calendar for the Western Church. Dionysius modified the Alexandrian system of dating, which used as its base the reign of Diocletian, for he did not want the years of history to be reckoned from the life of a persecutor of the church, but from the incarnation of Christ. The commencement of the Christian era was January 1, 754 A.U.C. (*anno urbis conditae* = from the foundation of the city [of Rome]) and Christ's birth was thought to have been on December 25th immediately preceding. So 754 A.U.C. became A.D. 1 in the calendar of Dionysius.

The years before this date are denoted by B.C. (before

Christ) and after by A.D. (*anno Domini* = in the year of the Lord) with no zero between 1 B.C. and A.D. 1. However, later research indicated that the latest year for Herod's death was 750 A.U.C. and Christ's birth, according to Matthew, occurred before Herod's death.[1] Hence, today it is generally recognized that the birth of Christ did not occur in A.D. 1 but some time before that.

As to how soon before A.D. 1 Christ was born, there is great divergence of opinion. Olmstead[2] dates it 20 B.C. and more recently Ogg dates it as early as 11 B.C.[3] On the other hand Filmer would probably date it somewhere between 3 and 1 B.C.[4] Hence there is a span of up to nineteen years.

In the broadest terms Luke 2:1 states that Christ was born in the reign of Caesar Augustus (who reigned from March 15, 44 B.C. to August 19, A.D. 14[5]). Since this is so broad, one needs to narrow the limits. In the attempt to arrive at a more specific date, it is essential to establish two concrete limits, the *termini a quo* (the earliest limiting point in time) and *ad quem* (the final limiting point in time). With respect to this, the *terminus ad quem* is the death of Herod the Great, and the *terminus a quo* is the census of Quirinius (Cyrenius).

TERMINUS AD QUEM: THE DEATH OF HEROD THE GREAT

According to Matthew 2:1 and Luke 1:5, Christ's birth came before Herod's death. Herod was proclaimed king of

[1] For more discussion on this, see Jack Finegan, *Handbook of Biblical Chronology* (Princeton, 1964), pp. 132-34; John Adam Robson, "Chronology: VIII Christian,"*Encyclopaedia Britannica,* V (14th ed., 1972), 728.

[2] A. T. Olmstead, "The Chronology of Jesus' Life," *Anglican Theological Review,* XXIV (January, 1942), 23-26.

[3] G. Ogg, "Chronology of the New Testament," *Peake's Commentary on the Bible,* ed. by Matthew Black (London, 1962), p. 728; G. Ogg, "Chronology of the New Testament," *The New Bible Dictionary,* ed. by J. D. Douglas (1962), p. 223.

[4] W. E. Filmer, "The Chronology of the Reign of Herod the Great," *The Journal of Theological Studies,* XVII (October, 1966), 283-98.

[5] Appian *Bella Civilia* ii. 149; Plutarch *Caesar* lxii-lxvii; Suetonius *Caesar* lxxxi. 2; Suetonius *Augustus* c. 1; Dio Cassius lvi. 30; Josephus *Antiquitates Judaicae* xviii. 2. 2 § 32; *Bellum Judaicum* ii. 9. 1 § 168 [hereafter Jos. *Ant.* and *BJ* respectively].

the Jews by the Roman Senate in late 40 B.C. by nomination of Antony and Octavian[6] and with the help of the Roman army he gained the possession of his domain in 37 B.C.[7] He reigned for thirty-seven years from the time he was made king or thirty-four years from the time of his possession of the land.[8]

According to Josephus, an eclipse of the moon occurred shortly before Herod's death.[9] It is the only eclipse ever mentioned by Josephus and this occurred on March 12/13, 4 B.C.[10] After his death there was the celebration of the Passover,[11] the first day of which would have occurred on April 11, 4 B.C.[12] Hence, his death occurred sometime between March 12th and April 11th. Since the thirty-fourth year of his reign would have begun on Nisan 1, 4 B.C. (March 29, 4 B.C.[13]), his death would have occurred some time between March 29 and April 11, 4 B.C.[14] Therefore, for these reasons, Christ could not have been born later than March/April of 4 B.C.

TERMINUS A QUO: THE CENSUS OF QUIRINIUS

According to Luke 2:1-5 a census was taken just before Christ's birth. Thus, Christ could not have been born before the census. The purpose of a census was to provide statistical data for the levy of taxes in the provinces. This census

---

[6]Jos. *Ant.* xiv. 14.4 §§ 381-85; *BJ* i. 14.4 §§ 282-85; cf. also Strabo xvi. 2. 46; Appian *Bella Civilia* v. 75; Tacitus *Historiae* v. 9.
[7]Jos. *Ant.* xiv. 16. 2 §§ 470-80; *BJ* i. 18. 2 §§ 349-52; Tacitus *Historiae* v. 9; Dio Cassius xlix. 22.
[8]Jos. *Ant.* xvii. 8. 1 § 191; *BJ* i. 33. 8 § 665.
[9]Jos. *Ant.* xvii. 6. 4 § 167.
[10]Emil Schürer, *The History of the Jewish People in the Age of Jesus Christ*, new English version rev. and ed. by Geza Vermes, Fergus Millar, and Matthew Black (Edinburgh, 1973), I, 326-28 n. 165.
[11]Jos. *BJ* ii. 1. 3 § 10; *Ant.* xvii. 9. 3 § 213.
[12]Richard A. Parker and Waldo H. Dubberstein, *Babylonian Chronology 626 B.C. — A.D. 75* (2nd ed.; Providence, 1956), p. 45.
[13]*Ibid.*
[14]Filmer, *(The Journal of Theological Studies,* XVII, 283-98) attempted to argue for January 1 B.C. for Herod's death. But his theory will not stand as demonstrated by Timothy D. Barnes, "The Date of Herod's Death," *The Journal of Theological Studies,* XIX (April, 1968), 204-9.

mentioned by Luke is one of the thorny problems of the New Testament and the major portion of this chapter will be concerned with it. Schürer states that Luke cannot be historically accurate because: (1) nothing is known in history of a general census in the time of Augustus; (2) in a Roman census Joseph would not have had to travel to Bethlehem, but would have registered in the principal town of his residence, and Mary would not have had to register at all; (3) no Roman census would have been made in Palestine during Herod's reign; (4) Josephus records nothing of a Roman census in Palestine in the time of Herod — rather the census of A.D. 6-7 was something new among the Jews; and (5) a census held under Quirinius could not have occurred during Herod's reign for Quirinius was not governor until after Herod's death.[15] As weighty as these objections may seem, they can be answered.

(1) *Census in Augustus' reign.* There is sufficient evidence of a census being taken periodically under the Republic and by Augustus in 28 B.C. and on subsequent occasions. In Gaul, where there was resistance, censuses were conducted in 27 and 12 B.C. and in Cyrene in 7 B.C.[16] In Egypt there were censuses taken in fourteen-year intervals begin-

---

[15]Schürer, I, 399-427. Cf. also Horst Braunert, "Der römische Provinzialzensus und der Schätungsbericht des Lukas-Evangeliums," *Historia,* VI (1957), 192-214; Hans Ulrich Instinsky, *Das Jahr der Geburt Christi* (München, 1957), pp. 11-73; J. Duncan M. Derrett, "Further Light on the Narratives of the Nativity," *Novum Testamentum,* XVII (April, 1975), 81-108. Recently Moehring has also argued that Luke is inaccurate historically and that the census is an apologetic device used by Luke to demonstrate that the Christian movement (along with Joseph's family) was obedient to the Roman government as opposed to the rebel movement of the Zealots, Horst R. Moehring, "The Census in Luke as an Apologetic Device," *Studies in the New Testament and Early Christian Literature,* ed. by David Edward Aune, *Supplements to Novum Testamentum,* XXXIII (Leiden, 1972), pp. 144-60. If it is an inaccurate historical account, how can it have any apologetic value? For a recent defense of Luke's accuracy cf. David J. Haxles, "The Roman Census & Jesus' Birth. Was Luke Correct?" *Buried History,* IX (December, 1973), 113-32; X (March, 1974), 17-31.
[16]G. H. Stevenson, "The Imperial Administration," *The Cambridge Ancient History,* ed. by S. A. Cook, F. E. Adcock, and M. P. Charlesworth (Cambridge, 1934), X, 192-93.

ning with 9 B.C.[17] Luke's statement: "In those days a decree
went out from Caesar Augustus that all the world was to be
taxed" has been challenged by those who claim that there
never was a single census of the entire Roman Empire.
However, is this what Luke meant? Probably not. What is
meant is that censuses were taken at different times in different provinces — Augustus being the first one in history to
order a census or tax assessment of the whole provincial
empire.[18] This is further substantiated by the fact that Luke
uses the present tense indicating that Augustus ordered censuses to be taken regularly rather than only one time.[19] Thus,
it is reasonable to believe that there was an order of a general
census in the time of Augustus.

(2) *Travel to home for a census.* According to Schürer,
Joseph as well as Mary would not have been compelled to go
to Bethlehem. Roman law states that the property owner had
to register for taxation in the district in which his land was
situated.[20] But there is a papyrus of A.D. 104 where the
prefect of Egypt ordered Egyptians to return to their home
so that the census might be carried out.[21] Since the Jews'
property was the property of the fathers' estates the Romans
would comply to the custom of laying claim to one's family
estate in order to assess it for taxation. Every person needed
to appear to be questioned so as to make a proper assessment
of his property. Because of this Mary would have needed to
go.[22] Since Mary's pregnancy was near its end, Joseph and
Mary may have wanted to go to Bethlehem because they
knew that Messiah would be born in Bethlehem (Mic. 5:1).

[17]Cf. W. M. Ramsay, *The Bearing of Recent Discoveries on the Trustworthiness of the New Testament* (4th ed.; London, 1920), pp. 255-74.
[18]A. N. Sherwin-White, *Roman Society and Roman Law in the New
Testament* (Oxford, 1963), p. 168.
[19]W. M. Ramsay, *Was Christ Born at Bethlehem?* (2nd ed.; London,
1898), pp. 123-24.
[20]Ulpian *Iustiniani Digesta* 1. 15. 4. 2.
[21]Adolf Deissmann, *Light from the Ancient East,* trans. by Lionel R. M.
Strachen (4th ed.; New York, 1927), pp. 270-71.
[22]Ethelbert Stauffer, *Jesus and His Story,* trans. by Dorothea M. Barton
(London, 1960), p. 35; cf. also Ramsay, *Bearing of Recent Discoveries,*
pp. 258-74; Ramsay, *Born at Bethlehem,* pp. 131-48.

Additionally, Joseph may not have wanted to leave her behind in Nazareth for fear that she would be treated with insults when the child was born.[23] Finally, one may conclude that going to their home for a census points to a time before Herod the Great's death and the division of his kingdom. It is highly implausible that after the division of the kingdom, the residents of Herod Antipas' territory (Nazareth) would go to Archelaus' territory (Bethlehem) for a census for purposes of taxation.[24]

(3) *Roman census in Herod's reign.* Schürer did not think that Augustus would have a census taken in Palestine during Herod's reign. Certainly Herod had enough autonomy as indicated by his being allowed to mint coins. However, the Romans did take a census in vassal kingdoms. In fact, in Venice a gravestone of a Roman officer was found which states that he was ordered by P. Sulpicius Quirinius to conduct a census of Apamea, a city of 117,000 inhabitants, located on the Orontes in Syria,[25] which was an autonomous city-state that minted its own copper coins.[26] In A.D. 36 under Tiberius a census was imposed on the client kingdom of Archelaus of Cappadocia.[27] Again, the powerful Nabatean kings in Petra, who had the right to mint coins were, it seems, obliged to have the Roman financial officers in their domain.[28] Another indication of Augustus' role in the finances of client kingdoms occurs when Herod's domain was divided among his three sons. Augustus ordered that the Samaritan's taxes should be reduced by one-fourth (because they had not revolted against Varus)[29] and this was before

[23]Norval Geldenhuys, *Commentary on the Gospel of Luke* (London, 1950), pp. 100-101.
[24]Bo Reicke, *The New Testament Era,* trans. by David E. Green (Philadelphia, 1968), p. 106.
[25]Cf. Stauffer, p. 32; Finegan, p. 237.
[26]A. R. Bellinger, *The Coins,* Final Report VI of *The Excavations at Dura-Europos,* ed. by M. I. Rostovtzeff, *et al.* (New Haven, 1949), p. 86, nos. 1832, 1833.
[27]Tacitus *Annales* vi. 41.
[28]Stauffer, pp. 31-32.
[29]Jos. *Ant.* xvii. 11. 4 § 319; *BJ* ii. 6. 3 § 96.

Samaria became a part of a Roman province.[30] Hence, it is seen that the Roman emperor became involved in taking censuses in the vassal kingdoms.

Normally, it seems that Herod collected his own taxes and paid tribute to Rome.[31] However, in 8/7 B.C. Herod came into disfavor with Augustus and was treated as a subject rather than a friend.[32] This would mean Herod's autonomy would be taken away. It is interesting to note that the people of Herod's domain took an oath of allegiance to Augustus and Herod[33] which points to a greater involvement of Augustus in Herod's realm. Herod was getting old and ill and he had much trouble with his sons who were struggling to acquire the throne. Hence, it would have been a good time for Augustus to have an assessment of the domain before Herod's death so as to prepare for the future rule of his realm. Therefore, since Augustus had taken censuses in other vassal kingdoms and since Herod had come into the emperor's disfavor as well as having troubles in his realm, it is more than probable that Augustus had conducted a census assessing Herod's kingdom while Herod was still alive.

(4) *No confusion of the censuses.* Schürer states that Josephus mentions nothing of a Roman census in Palestine in the time of Herod and that the census taken after Archelaus' deposition in A.D. 6 was something new and unheard of. However, the first part of the above objection is an argument from silence. There could have been a census with no disturbance and hence nothing worthwhile or significant to be mentioned by Josephus. No doubt the revolt with the census in A.D. 6 caused it to be recorded in Josephus[34] and in Acts 5:37. Ogg argues that since there is no revolt mentioned in Luke 2:2, this indicates that the first census by Quirinius was

[30]Alfred Plummer, *The Gospel according to S. Luke* (4th ed.; Edinburgh, 1905), p. 49.
[31]Cf. Harold W. Hoehner, *Herod Antipas* (Cambridge, 1972), pp. 298-300.
[32]Jos. *Ant.* xvi. 9. 3 § 290.
[33]Jos. *Ant.* xvii. 2. 4 § 42.
[34]Jos. *Ant.* xviii. 1. 1 §§ 1-10.

in A.D. 6-7.[35] But there are reasons for the revolt in A.D. 6-7. There was a Jewish and Samaritan delegation which made a formal complaint to the emperor asking that Archelaus be deposed.[36] They were sick of Herodian rule and probably wanted direct Roman rule. Subsequently Quirinius came to take a census which led to a revolt. This is understandable. First, the rebels may not have wanted direct Roman rule, hence disagreeing with the delegation. Second, the revolt was easier to start in A.D. 6 because Archelaus was summoned to Rome, leaving a vacuum in leadership in Palestine. A Roman census in Herod's time would have been conducted while he was in power. Third, there were Romans who came in to take the census which gave evidence that Rome was going to rule, whereas in Herod's time, he would have conducted the census according to the Jewish custom. Fourth, now that Herod's kingdom was divided, the census would be according to the normal Roman style spelled out in their law that the property owner had to register in the district in which his land was situated rather than going back to his ancestral home. The rebels would consider this another move on the part of the Romans to break down the national fiber of the Jews. Judas, the rebel leader, did not revolt because of taxes, but because there was no stable leadership and because he opposed direct Roman rule which would not be sensitive to the needs of the Jewish customs. Therefore, it is easy to see why most likely there would have been a peaceable census under Herod's rule.

(5) *Quirinius' governorship and the census.* Schürer says that a census held under Quirinius could not have occurred during Herod's reign for Quirinius was not governor until after Herod's death. This is the most formidable objection. This raises questions about the historicity of Luke. The critics say that Luke's dating of the birth of Christ with the census of Judea, which Josephus places after the deposition of Archelaus in A.D. 6, is a clear historical blun-

---

[35]George Ogg, "The Quirinius Question To-day," *The Expository Times,* LXXIX (May, 1968), 235.
[36]Jos. *Ant.* xvii. 13. 2 §§ 342-44; *BJ* ii. 7. 3 §§ 111-13.

der.[37] But certainly Luke was conscious of chronology in his works. This is seen, for example, in Luke 3:1 and 3:23. Luke was not ignorant of the census mentioned by Josephus which was conducted by Quirinius in A.D. 6-7 since he mentions it in Acts 5:37. He knew that Jesus was not born that late, for he states in Luke 1:5 that the births of John the Baptist and Jesus took place in the days of Herod. This certainly agrees with Matthew's chronology (Matt. 2:1). Also, Luke is consistent with himself in stating that Jesus was about thirty years of age when He began His ministry (Luke 3:23) which was shortly preceded by John the Baptist's that began in the fifteenth year of Tiberius (Luke 3:1-2). Since the fifteenth year of Tiberius can be dated around A.D. 27 to 29,[38] it would mean that if Christ were born in A.D. 6, He would only have been twenty-one to twenty-three years old, not about thirty years old.

Still, what does one do with Luke's statement about the census? Stauffer has argued strongly that there should be a distinction between the first stage of a census, namely, ἀπογραφή (the registration of taxable persons and objects) of which Luke speaks; and the final stage of a census ἀποτίμησις (the official assessment of the taxes) which is described by Josephus as occurring after Archelaus' deposition in A.D. 6.[39] But Stauffer's distinctions collapse when one looks at Josephus' account of the census in A.D. 6-7 where both terms are used in the same context[40] and in Acts 5:37 where the account of the same event uses the term ἀπογραφή.

On the basis of inscriptional evidence, Ramsay argues that Quirinius was governor of Syria twice, once from 11/10 to 8/7 B.C. and then a decade later (A.D. 6-7).[41] This has been questioned because this involves Quirinius as legate of Syria

[37]Cf. Reicke, pp. 106, 135-36.
[38]This question will be treated in chapter II.
[39]Stauffer, pp. 30-31; cf. also L. Dupraz, *De l'association de Tibère au principat à la naissance du Christ,* Vol. XLIII of *Studia Friburgensia* (Fribourg, 1966), pp. 143-220.
[40]Ἀπογραφή in Jos. *Ant.* xviii. 1.1 § 3 and ἀποτίμησις in xviii. 1.1 §§ 2, 4.
[41]Ramsay, *Bearing of Recent Discoveries,* pp. 275-300.

when he conquered the Homanadensians.[42] Some scholars argue that he was legate of Galatia when he was involved in the Homanadensian war.[43] Furthermore, the dating of this war is difficult to determine. Ramsay felt that the enrollment by Quirinius was made in 8-7 B.C., but argues that in Palestine it was delayed until around 6 B.C.[44] One can see that there are quite a few conditions which must be assumed before this theory works. This considerably weakens the case.

Sherwin-White argues for a double legateship of Quirinius. Quirinius was well-known in the Syrian area during the period around the time of Christ's birth, but he specifically thinks that Quirinius' first term was after Varus who was governor from 6 to 4 B.C.[45] Since it is unknown who was governor between Varus and Gaius Caesar (1 B.C. - A.D. 4), it is felt that Quirinius could have been governor at that time. However, this is after Herod the Great's death if one dates it in the spring of 4 B.C.

Another consideration is the one that was first proposed by Herwartus of the seventeeth century and revived in 1911 by Lagrange[46] and more recently by Heichelheim,[47] Turner,[48] and Bruce[49] by translating Luke 2:2 as following:

[42]Tacitus *Annales* iii. 48.
[43]Cf. Lily Ross Taylor, "Quirinius and the Census of Judaea," *The American Journal of Philology*, LIV (April, May, June, 1933), 120-33; Ronald Syme, "Galatia and Pamphylia under Augustus: the Governorships of Piso, Quirinius, and Silvanus," *Klio*, XXVII (1934), 131-38; A. G. Roos, "Die Quirinius-Inschrift," *Mnemosyne*, IV (1941), 306-18; Barbara Levick, *Roman Colonies in Southern Asia Minor* (Oxford, 1967), pp. 203-14.
[44]Ramsay, *Born at Bethlehem*, pp. 174-96.
[45]Sherwin-White, pp. 164-66.
[46]M.-J. Lagrange, "Où en est la question du recensement de Quirinius?" *Revue Biblique*, VIII (Janvier, 1911), 60-84.
[47]F. M. Heichelheim, "Roman Syria," *An Economic Survey of Ancient Rome*, ed. by Tenney Frank (Baltimore, 1938), IV, 160-62.
[48]Nigel Turner, *Grammatical Insights into the New Testament* (Edinburgh, 1965), pp. 23-24.
[49]F. F. Bruce, *New Testament History* (London, 1969), p. 32 n. 1. This is a change from his earlier view, see Frederick Fyvie Bruce, "Census," *Twentieth Century Encyclopedia of Religious Knowledge*, ed. by Lefferts A. Loetscher, I (1955), 222 and F. F. Bruce, "Quirinius," *The New Bible Dictionary*, ed. by J. D. Douglas (1962), p. 1069.

"This census was before that [census] when Quirinius was governor of Syria." Strictly speaking πρῶτος "first" is the superlative, meaning number one among at least three, while πρότερος "former" is the comparative form which compares only two. However, in later Greek the true comparative "πρότερος has surrendered the meaning 'the first of two' to πρῶτος and now means only 'earlier'."[50] Speaking classically this would have been the first census of a series, but hellenistically it could mean the first of two.[51] The examples cited of πρῶτος having a comparative force are John 1:15 and 30 (πρῶτός μου ἦν = "he was before me"), and the comparison is direct. In Luke 2:2 something has to be supplied, namely, "this census was earlier than [the census] when Quirinius was governor of Syria." Other examples of a concise statement where something has to be supplied are John 5:36 and 1 Corinthians 1:25. However, one notable difference between Luke 2:2 and the other passages cited is that Luke 2:2 has the participial phrase "when Quirinius was governor of Syria," which is cumbersome, namely, "This census was earlier than [the census] when Quirinius was governor of Syria."

Moving along the same line of argumentation, a better solution is the one suggested by Higgins. In John 15:18 the πρῶτος used adverbially is equivalent to πρό, that is, "It [the world] has hated me *before* it hated you." "If this is

---

[50]F. Blass and A. Debrunner, *A Greek Grammar of the New Testament and Other Early Christian Literature*, trans. by Robert W. Funk (Chicago, 1961), § 62; cf. also James Hope Moulton, *Prolegomena*, Vol. I of *A Grammar of New Testament Greek* (3rd ed.; Edinburgh, 1908), pp. 79, 107; A. T. Robertson, *A Grammar of the Greek New Testament in the Light of Historical Research* (4th ed.; New York, 1923), p. 669. Maximilian Zerwick, *Biblical Greek,* trans. adapted from the 4th Latin ed. by Joseph Smith (Rome, 1963), p. 50; Henry George Liddell and Robert Scott (comps.), *A Greek-English Lexicon,* new ed. rev. and augmented by Henry Stuart Jones (9th ed.; Oxford, 1940), p. 1535; Walter Bauer, *A Greek-English Lexicon of the New Testament and Other Early Christian Literature,* trans. and adaptation of the 4th rev. and augmented ed. by William F. Arndt and F. Wilbur Gingrich (Cambridge and Chicago, 1957), p. 733.
[51]Nigel Turner, *Syntax,* Vol. III of *A Grammar of New Testament Greek* (Edinburgh, 1963), p. 32.

conceded, there is no need to infer a compendious comparison, and πρώτη governs the participial phrase. The Greek means, 'This census took place before Quinirius was governor of Syria'. Luke is not distinguishing an earlier census from one during the governorship of Quirinius, but is merely stating that the census at the time of the nativity took place some time before Quirinius held office."[52] This gives good sense to the passage at hand. As stated above, Quirinius was governor of Syria in A.D. 6-7 and possibly also, as Sherwin-White has argued, in 3-2 B.C. If this has reference to his governorship in A.D. 6-7 then this census is before the governorship when he had conducted the well-known census mentioned in Josephus and Luke. On the other hand, this also fits nicely if he were governor in 3-2 B.C.; for Luke is then stating that just before Quirinius was governor in Syria in 3-2 B.C. there was a census in Herod's domains.

The exact date of the census cannot be determined with precision. However, it is reasonable to think that the census would have been after Herod came into disfavor with Augustus in 8/7 B.C. More specifically it was probably after Herod's execution of his sons Alexander and Aristobulus in 7 B.C. when there was an intense struggle for the throne by his other sons which resulted in Herod's changing his will three times before his death in the spring of 4 B.C.[53] In 7 B.C. Herod named Antipater as sole heir, and then in 5 B.C. a new will was drawn up, making Antipas the heir. Finally, five days before Herod's death Antipater was executed and a final will was drawn up, naming Archelaus as king of the whole realm. Furthermore, not only were there the intrigues within the household, but Herod's illness became more intense. His death was imminent. With such instability and such a bad state of health, it would have been an opportune time for Augustus to have had a census taken in order to assess the situation before Herod's death. It must also be noted that Augustus was well aware of the situation in Palestine, be-

[52]A. J. B. Higgins, "Sidelights on Christian Beginnings in the Graeco-Roman World," *The Evangelical Quarterly*, XLI (October, 1969), 200-201.
[53]Cf. Hoehner, pp. 269-76.

cause each time Herod changed his will and each time he wanted to get rid of one of his sons, he had to ask the emperor's permission. Therefore, a census within the last year or two of Herod's reign would have been reasonable, and in fact, most probable.

The exact year of this census, which would mark the *terminius a quo* of Christ's birth, is difficult to pinpoint but it was probably taken sometime between 6 and 4 B.C., preferably the latter part of this span of time. This fits well with both Matthew's and Luke's chronologies, which seem to indicate that the census and Christ's birth were shortly before Herod's death.

OTHER CHRONOLOGICAL CONSIDERATIONS

Having narrowed the date of Christ's birth between 6 and 4 B.C., other chronological notes are to be considered.

"Not yet fifty years old." In John 8:57 the Jews said to Jesus, "You are not yet fifty years old." Irenaeus held that Jesus was in His forties, for if Jesus were in His thirties they would have said, "You are not yet forty years old."[54] Ogg takes this chronological note in John 8:57 seriously and doubts that Luke 3:23 can serve any chronological purpose. Ogg, then, dates the birth of Christ somewhere between 11 and 9 B.C.[55] But certainly the opposite is more likely. Luke 3:23 is a precise statement whereas John 8:57 indicates that the Jews were emphasizing Jesus' youth in contrast to His claim that He existed before Abraham. Therefore, John 8:57 is not helpful in trying to narrow the date of Christ's birth.

"Two years old and under." In Matthew 2:16 Herod saw that he had been tricked by the Magi[56] when they did not return to report the location of Jesus and consequently

[54]Irenaeus *Adversus Haereses* ii. 22. 6.
[55]Ogg, *Peake's Commentary on the Bible*, p. 728.
[56]The star which the Magi followed does not give any help in pinpointing the date of Christ's birth. For a discussion of the star, see Kenneth D. Boa, "The Star of Bethlehem" (unpublished Th.M. thesis, Dallas Theological Seminary, 1972).

Herod slew all the male children two years old and under in Bethlehem and its surrounding area. The question arises whether Matthew is speaking of the same time as Luke or a later time. Madison attempts to demonstrate that the Magi visited Christ when He was about two years of age by noting that the Lukan narrative uses the term βρέφος (2:12) which is used to refer to an unborn, a newborn child, or an infant whereas Matthew uses the words παιδίον (2:8, 9, 11, 13 *bis,* 14, 20 *bis,* 21) and παῖς (2:16) which are used of a child that is at least one year old rather than an infant. The fact that the wise men came to the house (in Matthew's account) rather than a manger (in Luke's account) would also indicate that Jesus was older when Herod slew the children.[57] Thus Luke is talking about the time of Christ's birth whereas Matthew is talking about two years after Christ's birth.

However, the distinction is not so clear-cut as Madison would have one to believe. The term παιδίον is used of infants (Luke 1:59, 66, 76; 2:17, 27; John 16:21; Heb. 11:23) and βρέφος is used of a young child (2 Tim. 3:15). The word παῖς is used in the New Testament of a child six out of twenty-four times (the other eighteen occurrences speak of a servant). In the Old Testament the meaning "servant" is almost unanimous. In Matthew 2:16 παῖς would fall into the same age category as παιδίον since the latter term is used nine times in the same context. Furthermore, to say that Jesus was no longer an infant because the Magi visited Him in a house rather than a stable is quite weak. Certainly they would have moved to a house as soon as it was possible. Indeed the tone of Matthew 2:1 is that the Magi visited Christ soon after His birth. That Herod killed children up to two years old was only to be sure he got Jesus. This is not out of character with Herod. Therefore, the slaying of the children soon after Christ's birth is tenable.

"About thirty years of age." Luke 3:23 states that Jesus began His ministry when He was about thirty years of age.

---

[57]Leslie P. Madison, "Problems of Chronology in the Life of Christ" (unpublished Th.D. dissertation, Dallas Theological Seminary, 1963), pp. 25-27.

This was preceded by the commencement of John the Baptist's ministry which according to Luke 3:1 occurred in the fifteenth year of Tiberius. These passages will be studied in chapter II in greater detail, but suffice it to state here, the fifteenth year of Tiberius was around (depending on how one reckons it) A.D. 27 to 29. How much latitude can one allow for ὡσεί "about" thirty years of age? It seems that no more than two or three years on either side of thirty is feasible. Hence, if Christ's ministry began in A.D. 27 or 29, His birth would have had to be no earlier than 5 B.C. and it seems that late 5 B.C. or early 4 B.C. best satisfies all the evidence.[58]

Conclusion. Having considered some of these chronological notes, it seems the evidence would lead one to conclude that Christ's birth occurred sometime in late 5 B.C. or early 4 B.C.

THE DAY OF CHRIST'S BIRTH

There have been lengthy discussions on the day of Christ's birth.[59] Those who have studied the question, have advocates for almost every month of the year. Since it is beyond the scope of this chapter to do a detailed study of the day of Christ's birth, only the two traditional dates will be mentioned.

The traditional date for the birth of Christ from as early as Hippolytus (*ca.* A.D. 165-235)[60] has been December 25th. In the Eastern Church January 6th was the date for not only Christ's birth, but also the arrival of the Magi on Christ's second birthday, His baptism in His twenty-ninth year, and the sign at Cana in His thirtieth year. However, Chrysostom (A.D. 345-407) in 386 stated that December 25th is the correct date and hence it became the official date for Christ's birth in

[58]Finegan (p. 248) comes to the same date though he uses some different data.
[59]*Ibid.*, pp. 248-59; F. C. Conybeare, "The History of Christmas," *The American Journal of Theology*, III (January, 1899), 1-21; Kirsopp Lake, "Christmas," *Encyclopedia of Religion and Ethics*, ed. by James Hastings, III (1910), 601-8; J. Lamar Jackson, "Christmas," *Review and Expositor*, XLI (October, 1944), 388-96; E. O. James, *Seasonal Feasts and Festivals* (New York, 1961), pp. 228-32.
[60]Hippolytus *Comentarii in Danielem* iv. 23. 3.

the Eastern Church (January 6th was still considered the day for the manifestations of the coming of the Magi, the baptism, and the sign at Cana).[61]

Although the exact date may not be pinpointed it seems that there is "a relatively old tradition of a midwinter birth, therefore a date in December or January is not in itself unlikely."[62]

The one objection raised for the winter date is the fact of the shepherds attending their flock in the night (Luke 2:8). Usually, it is noted, the sheep were taken into enclosures from November until March and were not in the fields at night.[63] However, this is not conclusive evidence against December being the time of Christ's birth for the following reasons. First, it could have been a mild winter and hence the shepherds would have been outside with their sheep. Second, it is not at all certain that sheep were brought under cover during the winter months.[64] Third, it is true that during the winter months the sheep were brought in from the wilderness. The Lukan narrative states that the shepherds were around Bethlehem (rather than the wilderness), thus indicating that the nativity was in the winter months. Finally, the Mishnah[65] implies that the sheep around Bethlehem were outside all year, and those that were worthy for the Passover offerings were in the fields thirty days before the feast — which would be as early as February — one of the coldest and rainiest months of the year.[66] Therefore, a December date for the nativity is acceptable.[67]

---

[61]Finegan, p. 258. Cf. also Oscar Cullmann, *The Early Church*, ed. by A. J. B. Higgins (Philadelphia, 1956), pp. 19-36.
[62]Finegan, p. 259.
[63]A. T. Robertson, *A Harmony of the Gospels for Students of the Life of Christ* (New York, 1922), p. 267; Madison, pp. 53-54.
[64]Plummer, p. 55; William F. Arndt, *The Gospel according to St. Luke* (St. Louis, 1956), pp. 80-81.
[65]Shekalim vii. 4.
[66]Cf. Denis Baly, *The Geography of the Bible* (New York, 1957), pp. 41-66.
[67]Cf. also Alfred Edersheim, *The Life and Times of Jesus the Messiah* (3rd ed.; London, 1886), I, 186-87; Samuel J. Andrews, *The Life of Our Lord upon the Earth* (4th ed.; New York, 1891), pp. 12-21, 87-89.

In conclusion, the exact date of the birth of Christ is difficult to know with finality. However, a midwinter date is most likely.

CONCLUSION

It is clear that Christ was born before Herod the Great's death and after the census. In looking at the birth narratives of Matthew and Luke one would need to conclude that Christ was born of Mary within a year or two of Herod's death. In looking to some of the other chronological notations in the Gospels, the evidence led to the conclusion that Christ was born in the winter of 5/4 B.C. Although the exact date of Christ's birth cannot be known, either December, 5 B.C., or January, 4 B.C., is most reasonable.

From Matthew and Luke it seems that Jesus and Mary went from Nazareth to Bethlehem for the census (Luke 2:4-5). Jesus was born in Bethlehem (Matt. 2:1; Luke 2:6). There was a visitation by the shepherds (Luke 2:8-20) and the Magi (Matt. 2:1-12). Jesus was circumcised, presented to God in Jerusalem, and then returned to Nazareth (Luke 2:21-39). Because of a dream in Bethlehem, they went to Egypt until Herod's death and then returned to Nazareth (Matt. 2:13-23). At twelve years of age Jesus went to Jerusalem and then returned to Nazareth (Luke 2:40-52).

Chapter II

The Commencement of Christ's Ministry

Having concluded in the previous chapter that the birth of Christ occurred either in December, 5 B.C., or January, 4 B.C., the next important chronological aspects of the life of Christ are the commencement and duration of His public ministry. This chapter will deal with the first area and the next chapter with the duration of His ministry. Concerning the year in which our Lord began His ministry, there are four passages of Scripture to be considered.

"IN THE FIFTEENTH YEAR OF THE REIGN OF TIBERIUS"

Luke 3:1-3 mentions that it was in the fifteenth year of the reign of Tiberius that the Word of God came to John the Baptist in the wilderness and that he went into all the region around the Jordan preaching the baptism of repentance for the forgiveness of sins. At the time John was baptizing the people, he also baptized Jesus which marked the commencement of His ministry. Thus, Jesus' ministry commenced after the opening of John's ministry. Since Luke dates the beginning of John's activity with chronological notes of secular history (which he does not do for the beginning of Christ's ministry), it is necessary to determine when John embarked on his ministry.[1] This will establish the *terminus a quo* (the earliest limiting point in time) for Christ's ministry.

---

[1]Portions of this section are reproduced from Harold W. Hoehner, *Herod Antipas* (Cambridge, 1972), Appendix VII, pp. 307-12. Permission was granted by Cambridge University Press.

29

In Luke 3:1-2[2] six chronological notations[3] are listed. Five of these give only the broadest limits: (1) Pilate was prefect of Judea from A.D. 26 to late 36 or early 37;[4] (2) Herod Antipas was deposed in A.D. 39;[5] (3) Philip died in A.D. 34;[6] (4) Lysanias, tetrarch of Abilene, cannot be dated;[7] and (5) Caiaphas was high priest from A.D. 18 until not later than the Passover of A.D. 37.[8] Hence, the broad limits for the begin-

[2]It is thought by Grant that the reason for this chronological notice was to prevent the chronological confusion respecting the Lord's ministry which was so evident in the following centuries. Grant thinks this confusion had already begun in the first century, as is seen in John 8:57 (Robert M. Grant, "The Occasion of Luke III:1-2," *The Harvard Theological Review*, XXXIII [April, 1940], 151-54). However, it is doubtful if John 8:57 was intended to serve as a chronological landmark. Moreover, the accuracy of Luke 3:1 cannot be challenged (A. N. Sherwin-White, *Roman Society and Roman Law in the New Testament* [Oxford, 1963], pp. 166-67).

[3]Similarly Thucydides introduces his account of the Peloponnesian Wars by a sextuple dating, Thucydides ii. 2. 1 (cf. also Polybius i. 3. 1-5). Luke may have taken over a form used by secular historiographers, who used to make prominent important events, especially those with which the narrative begins, by means of circumstantial datings and synchronisms (E. Schwartz, "Noch einmal der Tod der Söhne Zebedaei," *Zeitschrift für die neutestamentliche Wissenschaft*, XI [Mai, 1910], 102).

[4]Emil Schürer, *The History of the Jewish People in the Age of Jesus Christ*, new English version rev. and ed. by Geza Vermes, Fergus Millar, and Matthew Black (Edinburgh, 1973), I, 388 n. 145. Numismatically it could not have been before A.D. 26, cf. P. L. Hedley, "Pilate's Arrival in Judaea," *The Journal of Theological Studies*, XXXV (January, 1934), 56-58. Smallwood thinks that Josephus' figure of ten years (*Ant.* xviii. 4. 2 § 89) is a round number and thus dates his departure sometime between mid-December 36 and the end of February 37, cf. E. Mary Smallwood, "The Date of the Dismissal of Pontius Pilate from Judaea," *The Journal of Jewish Studies*, V, No. 1 (1954), 12-14, 19-21. See also Hoehner, Appendix VIII, pp. 313-16.

[5]Jos. *Ant.* xviii. 7. 1-2 §§ 240-56; Hoehner, pp. 260-63.

[6]Jos. *Ant.* xviii. 4. 6 § 106; Schürer, I, 340 n. 10; Hoehner, p. 251 and n. 1.

[7]The inscription which records a temple dedication by the freedman of Lysanias the tetrarch (*Corpus Inscriptionum Graecarum*, 4521) is dated between A.D. 14 and 29. For a discussion of the problem, see Schürer, Appendix I, pp. 565-70; John Martin Creed, *The Gospel according to St. Luke* (London, 1930), Additional Note, pp. 307-9; George Ogg, *The Chronology of the Public Ministry of Jesus* (Cambridge, 1940), pp. 171-72.

[8]Jos. *Ant.* xviii. 2. 2 § 35; 4. 3 § 95. Joachim Jeremias, *Jerusalem in the Time of Jesus*, trans. from the 3rd German ed. (1962) and rev. in 1967 by

ning of John's ministry are A.D. 26 and the Passover of A.D. 37. The one precise date is the fifteenth year of Tiberius, and this may be interpreted in five different ways.

RECKONING FROM TIBERIUS' CO-REGENCY

The first method of reckoning to be considered is that Luke was counting from the decree by which Tiberius became co-regent with Augustus.[9] On the basis of Velleius Paterculus ii. 121, Mommsen dates the decree at the end of A.D. 11[10] which would make A.D. 25/26 the fifteenth year of Tiberius. Hence, one can see that this method of reckoning allows for an early date for the commencement of John's ministry. But this method is to be rejected because there is no evidence, either from historical documents or coins, for its employment[11] whereas there is abundant evidence that

---

F. H. and C. H. Cave (Philadelphia, 1969), p. 195 n. 153; Hoehner, Appendix VIII, pp. 313-16. Luke also mentions the high priesthood of Annas. Although historically he was the high priest during A.D. 6-15 (Jos. *Ant.* xviii. 2. 1, 2 §§ 26, 34), he was not the high priest jointly with his son-in-law Caiaphas. However, since he was the powerful figure behind Annas, it may explain the reason for Luke's inclusion.

[9]For a discussion on this argument, see Karl Wieseler, *Beiträge zur richtigen Würdigung der Evangelien und der evangelischen Geschichte* (Gotha, 1869), pp. 195-96; W. M. Ramsay, *Was Christ Born at Bethlehem?* (2nd ed.; London, 1898), pp. 199-202, 221; Theodore Zahn, *Das Evangelium des Lucas* (Leipzig, 1913), pp. 183-88; Leslie P. Madison, "Problems of Chronology in the Life of Christ" (unpublished Th.D. dissertation, Dallas Theological Seminary, 1963), pp. 64-70.

[10]Theodore Mommsen, *Römisches Staatsrecht* (3rd ed.; Leipzig, 1887), II, ii, 1159 n. 3.

[11]Frederic W. Madden, *Coins of the Jews* (London, 1881), p. 177 n. 1; Karl Wieseler, *A Chronological Synopsis of the Four Gospels,* trans. by Edmund Venables (2nd ed., London, 1877), p. 172. Note Wieseler abandoned his position later in life, cf. Wieseler, *Beiträge,* pp. 177-96. For a thorough discussion on this, see Hermann Dieckmann, "Die effektive Mitregenschaft des Tiberius," *Klio,* XV, Heft 3/4 (1918), 339-75; J. K. Fotheringham, "The Evidence of Astronomy and Technical Chronology for the Date of the Crucifixion," *The Journal of Theological Studies,* XXXV (April, 1934), 151-52. Even for those who hold to the co-regency theory there is no agreement as to the beginning of the co-regency, cf. Ogg, pp. 174-83.

Tiberius reckoned his first year after the death of Augustus.[12] Any theory that has to distort the normal sense of the text is already suspect.

RECKONING FROM NISAN

The second method is that Luke reckoned from Nisan 1. This would make the first year of Tiberius last from August 19, A.D. 14[13] to Nisan 1, A.D. 15, and his fifteenth year from Nisan 1, 28 to Nisan 1, 29,[14] or April 15, 28 to April 4, 29.[15] It is felt by some of the adherents of this method that Luke was drawing on a source from John the Baptist's circle, which would have used the Jewish method of reckoning. The regnal years of their rulers commenced with Nisan 1.[16] Without any supporting evidence Ogg assumes this to be true. Although the Mishnaic tractate Rosh ha-Shanah specifically states that the regnal years were reckoned from Nisan 1,[17] a discussion on this in the Talmud shows that it was not universally accepted. After a considerable discussion it is decided that the kings of Israel were reckoned from Nisan 1 and the non-Israelite kings from Tishri 1, citing Nehemiah 1:1 and 2:1 as proof texts.[18] Rabbi Joseph objects by showing that this was not always the case. One cannot therefore count on

[12]E.g., Josephus states that Tiberius had reigned twenty-two years and five or six months (Jos. *Ant.* xviii. 6. 10 § 224; *BJ* ii. 9. 6 § 180) when reckoning backwards from his death of March 16, A.D. 37 would come to A.D. 14 for the first year of his reign. Also, according to Josephus, Philip the Tetrarch died when he had reigned for thirty-seven years which was the twentieth year of Tiberius' reign (Jos. *Ant.* xviii. 4. 6 § 106). Since Philip's death was in A.D. 34, Tiberius' first year would be A.D. 14 and not A.D. 11 or 12. Many more examples could be cited, see also nn. 11 and 13.
[13]The date marks the death of Augustus, Appian *Bella Civilia* ii. 149; Plutarch *Caesar* lxii-lxvii; Suetonius *Caesar* lxxxi. 2; Suetonius *Augustus* c. 1; Dio Cassius lvi. 30; Jos. *Ant.* xviii. 2. 2 § 32; *BJ* ii. 9. 1 § 168.
[14]Ogg, pp. 200-201.
[15]Richard A. Parker and Waldo H. Dubberstein, *Babylonian Chronology 626 B.C. — A.D. 75* (2nd ed.; Providence, 1956), p. 46.
[16]Ogg, pp. 196-200.
[17]Rosh ha-Shanah i. 1.
[18]Babylonian Talmud: Rosh ha-Shanah 3a-b, 8a; for a discussion of this, see Jack Finegan, *Handbook of Biblical Chronology* (Princeton, 1964), pp. 88-91.

Talmudic sources for a settled method of reckoning regnal years.[19]

Neither is it any help to see how the reckoning was calculated during the Maccabean times, for both Nisan and Tishri New Years were used. While 2 Maccabees always uses the Seleucid era (which reckons from October), 1 Maccabees seems to imply, although not at all clearly, that the author used the years beginning with Nisan when following Palestinian sources, and years beginning with Tishri when following a Syrian source.[20] Frank thinks both books reckon according to the Seleucid method, but that 1 Maccabees started year 1 in autumn 313 B.C. whereas 2 Maccabees started year 1 in 312 B.C.[21] In fact he believes in the Talmudic teaching (mentioned in the previous paragraph), that non-Jewish kings were reckoned from Tishri, and that this has reference to the Seleucid era.[22] The two books of Maccabees could be used as evidence for a Nisan 1 reckoning only if one agrees with Bickermann's or Dancy's theory.[23] Weightier is the evidence in favor of a Tishri 1 reckoning, but it cannot be pressed too far.

If one goes back to Old Testament times to determine regnal years, as Ogg does, one cannot conclude as he does that the Jews reckoned from Nisan 1. In fact, reckoning in the Old Testament varied a great deal in respect to both Hebrew and foreign kings. Thus it is difficult to determine whether they used the accession-year system (the first year of a king's reign begins on the first day of the new year after he became king) or the non-accession-year (the first year of

[19]Babylonian Talmud: Rosh ha-Shanah 3*b*; cf. Julian Morgenstern, "The New Year for Kings," *Occident and Orient,* ed. by Bruno Schindler (London, 1936), pp. 439-40.
[20]Bickerman, "Makkabäerbücher," *Realencyclopädie der klassischen Altertumswissenschaft,* ed. by A. Pauly and Georg Wissowa, XIV, 1 (1928), 781-84; J. C. Dancy, *A Commentary on 1 Maccabees* (Oxford, 1954), pp. 50-51.
[21]Edgar Frank, *Talmudic and Rabbinical Chronology* (New York, 1956), pp. 30-32.
[22]*Ibid.,* p. 35.
[23]As does Fotheringham, *The Journal of Theological Studies,* XXXV, 154.

the king is that portion of the year between his accession and the first day of the new year), and whether they reckoned from Nisan or Tishri.[24] Schürer feels that the Nisan system was used by Josephus for calculating the rule of Herod the Great.[25] But would Luke, a Gentile, use that system when writing to a Roman official? An interpretation such as this seems unlikely.

RECKONING FROM TISHRI

The third method is that used by Syria from the time of Augustus to Nerva. According to this the regnal years of the Roman emperors were reckoned from Tishri 1 as were those of the old Syro-Seleucids.[26] Thus, the first year of Tiberius would have extended from August 19, A.D. 14 to Tishri 1, 14, and his fifteenth year from Tishri 1, 27 to Tishri 1, 28;[27] that is, from September 21, 27 to October 8, 28.[28] The adherents of this view believe that since Luke was from Antioch,[29] he would have calculated the reigns of emperors according to

[24]For a discussion on these problems, see Edwin R. Thiele, *The Mysterious Numbers of the Hebrew Kings* (2nd ed.; Grand Rapids, 1965), pp. 16-38, 161.
[25]Schürer, I, 326-28 n. 165.
[26]Mommsen, II, ii, 802-4; Martin Dibelius, *From Tradition to Gospel*, trans. by Bertram Lee Woolf (2nd ed.; London, 1934), pp. 293-94. For a discussion of the Syrian calendars, see Finegan, pp. 61-68.
[27]Conrad Cichorius, "Chronologisches zum Leben Jesu," *Zeitschrift für die neutestamentliche Wissenschaft*, XXII (Juni, 1923), 17-19; Gustav Hölscher, "Die Hohenpriesterliste bei Josephus und die evangelische Chronologie," *Sitzungsberichte der Heidelberger Akademie der Wissenschaften — Philosophisch-historische Klasse*, XXX (Heidelberg, 1940), 27; Carl H. Kraeling, "Olmstead's Chronology of the Life of Jesus," *Anglican Theological Review*, XXIV (October, 1942), 346; Günther Bornkamm, *Jesus of Nazareth*, trans. by Irene and Fraser McLuskey with James M. Robinson (London, 1960), p. 45; George B. Caird, "The Chronology of the NT," *The Interpreter's Dictionary of the Bible*, ed. by George Arthur Buttrick, *et al.*, I (1962), 601.
[28]Parker and Dubberstein, p. 46.
[29]William Mitchell Ramsay, *St. Paul the Traveller and the Roman Citizen* (14th ed.; London, 1920), pp. 389-90; David Smith, *The Life and Letters of St. Paul* (London, 1919), Appendix IV, pp. 667-70; Hoehner, pp. 231-32 n. 9.

the calendar with which he was familiar.[30] Also, the official Jewish New Year, except possibly during the exilic period, commenced with the autumn equinox (especially after Nehemiah's reformation).[31] Would it not be natural to reckon regnal years from the New Year? Moreover, this method agrees well with other chronological factors in the life of Jesus. If Jesus was born around the winter of 5/4 B.C.,[32] then the beginning of His ministry could have been soon after the beginning of John's, possibly before the Passover of A.D. 28 (John 2:13). At this time He would have been only thirty or thirty-one, which fits well with the statement that He was "about thirty years of age" at the commencement of His ministry (Luke 3:23). Also, if Jesus indeed died on April 7, A.D. 30 it would allow at least three Passovers (John 2:13; 6:4; 11:55) to be included.[33] However, this limits Jesus' ministry to a little over two years. John's Gospel requires at least three years as will be seen in the discussion of the duration of Christ's ministry in the next chapter.

RECKONING FROM THE JULIAN CALENDAR

The fourth opinion is that Luke used the Julian Calendar. If one reckons according to the non-accession-year

[30]William M. Ramsay, "Numbers, Hours, Years, and Dates," *A Dictionary of the Bible,* ed. by James Hastings, *et al.,* Extra Volume (1904), 481; Cichorius, *Zeitschrift für die neutestamentliche Wissenschaft,* XXII, 18-19; Kraeling, *Anglican Theological Review,* XXIV, 344-46.
[31]J. F. McLaughlin, "New Year," *The Jewish Encyclopedia,* ed. by I. Singer, *et al.,* IX (1895), 254-56; Julian Morgenstern, "New Year," *The Interpreter's Dictionary of the Bible,* ed. by George Arthur Buttrick, *et al.,* III (1962), 544-46; Julian Morgenstern, "Year," *The Interpreter's Dictionary of the Bible,* ed. by George Arthur Buttrick, *et al.,* IV (1962), 923-24. Also, cf. Jos. *Ant.* i. 3. 3 §§ 80-81; J. Wellhausen, *Prolegomena zur Geschichte Israels* (6th ed.; Berlin, 1905), pp. 103-7; Israel Abrahams, "Time," *A Dictionary of the Bible,* ed. by James Hastings, *et al.,* IV (1902), 763-65.
[32]See Chapter I.
[33]Kraeling, *Anglican Theological Review,* XXIV, 346. Jeremias uses this method, cf. Joachim Jeremias, *The Eucharistic Words of Jesus,* trans. by Norman Perrin (3rd ed.; London, 1966), p. 39 n. 1.

system, then Tiberius' first year was from August 19 to December 31, 14 and his fifteenth year was from January 1 to December 31, 28. However, if one reckons according to the accession-year system the August 19 to December 31, 14, is considered the accession year and January 1 to December 31, 15, is considered Tiberius' first year of reign. Thus, his fifteenth year would have been from January 1 to December 31, 29. The use of the Julian Calendar and the reckoning according to the accession-year system was employed by Roman historians such as Tacitus and Suetonius.[34] The chief argument for this view of reckoning is that since the combined work of Luke-Acts is addressed to Theophilus (Luke 1:3) who is saluted as κράτιστε, a term Luke otherwise employs only as a form of address to a Roman official (Acts 23:26; 24:3; 26:25), it is probable therefore that the writing is addressed to Roman readers or to those under Roman dominion, who would be familiar with the Julian Calendar.[35]

RECKONING FROM TIBERIUS' REGNAL YEAR

The fifth opinion is that Luke used the normal Roman method of reckoning, according to which Tiberius' fifteenth year would have run from August 19, 28 to August 18, 29. Lewin states: "The reign of Tiberius, as beginning from 19th Aug. A.D. 14, was as well-known a date in the time of Luke as the reign of Queen Victoria in our own day, and that no single case has ever been or can be produced in which the years of Tiberius were reckoned in any other way."[36] The biggest objection to this view is that it would be too complicated and confusing to reckon according to dynastic years.[37] However, on the other hand, since Luke was addressing a Roman official it is plausible to think that he would have been familiar with dynastic years.

[34]For a discussion of this, see Finegan, pp. 271-72.
[35]*Ibid.*, p. 273.
[36]Thomas Lewin, *Fasti Sacri or a Key to the Chronology of the New Testament* (London, 1865), p. liii.
[37]Benedictus Niese, "Zur Chronologie des Josephus," *Hermes,* XXVIII, Heft 2 (1893), 210-11; Ogg, p. 187.

CONCLUSION

In conclusion, of the five methods, the first one is unacceptable and the second one is unlikely. If one were to accept A.D. 30 as the crucifixion date, then the third method would be the most probable. This would mean that the commencement of John the Baptist's ministry would have been between September 21, 27, and October 8, 28. This allows for Jesus' ministry to be a little more than two years. However, if one thinks that Jesus was crucified in A.D. 33, then either of the last two methods would be most probable, and would make the beginning of John's ministry between August 19, 28, and December 31, 29. The present author thinks that Christ's ministry was at least three years in duration and that Christ's crucifixion was in A.D. 33.[38] Therefore, either of the last two methods satisfies the requirements of the biblical narratives and both methods were used for reckoning in that day. Hence, it means that John the Baptist's ministry began sometime in A.D. 29.

From the Gospels one receives the impression that it was not long after John's ministry commenced that Jesus was baptized and began His ministry. If we accept the conclusion that John's ministry began sometime in A.D. 29, it is reasonable to suppose that Jesus' ministry also began in that same year or shortly thereafter.

"ABOUT THIRTY YEARS OF AGE"

In the same chapter Luke (3:23) mentions that at the commencement of His ministry, Jesus was "about thirty years of age." Since in the previous chapter it was concluded that Jesus was born around December, 5 B.C./January, 4 B.C., do the solutions mentioned in the above section agree with Luke 3:1-2? If one accepts the third solution in the above section and also has Jesus' baptism shortly before the Passover of A.D. 28 then He would have been only thirty or thirty-one years of age when He began His ministry. With both the fourth and the fifth solutions, it is possible for John to have baptized Christ early in A.D. 29 (with the fifth view

[38]Both of these assertions will be treated in chapters III and V respectively.

Christ could have been baptized in the autumn of A.D. 28) and to have Christ's ministry begin shortly before the Passover of A.D. 29. This would mean that Christ would have been around thirty-one or thirty-two years of age at the beginning of His ministry. However, it seems more plausible (using either the fourth or fifth solution) for John to have baptized Jesus sometime in A.D. 29 and to have the commencement of Christ's ministry sometime before the Passover of A.D. 30 which means that Christ would have been around thirty-two or thirty-three. This view is more acceptable for the following three reasons. First, it does not require a quick succession of events in such a short span of time in John's ministry. Second, it allows for Christ's ministry to be at least three years in duration. Third, the fact that Luke used the term "about" (ὡσεί) indicates that Jesus was not exactly thirty years of age when He began His ministry. Of course, how far one is allowed to stretch the limits of the term "about" is not known. One would think no more than two or three years from the time stated. To know exactly the time of the year when either John or Jesus began their respective ministries is not possible. However, it is conceivable that John began his ministry in the early part of A.D. 29 and that Jesus was baptized sometime in the summer or autumn of A.D. 29. If this is true then Jesus would have been thirty-two years of age with His thirty-third birthday approaching in December of A.D. 29 or January of A.D. 30.

"Forty-Six Years to Build This Temple"

The first recorded visit of Christ to Jerusalem after His baptism is found in John 2:13 — 3:21. At this time Jesus cleansed the temple and the Jews asked for a sign for His authority to do such a thing. He answered, "Destroy this temple, and in three days I will raise it up." The Jews replied, "It has taken forty-six years to build this temple, and you will raise it in three days?" Two extreme views must be avoided. On the one hand one cannot say that the Jews were referring to the temple constructed by Solomon or Zerubbabel for the demonstrative pronoun οὗτος "this" points to the actual temple that was existing there at that time. On the other hand the Jews were not saying that the entire Herodian temple was completed in forty-six years for that did not take place until Albinus' procuratorship in A.D. 62-64.[39] What, then, did the Jews mean in John 2:20?

CORBISHLEY'S THEORY

Josephus states in one place that Herod began to rebuild the temple in his eighteenth year[40] while in another place he says it was in his fifteenth year.[41] Corbishley says that these two figures can be reconciled by the fact that the first reference is reckoning from the time when the Roman Senate pronounced Herod king in 40 B.C. while the second reference is reckoned from the time he actually became king in 37 B.C. This means the temple was begun in 23/22 B.C. Corbishley continues his argumentation by showing that according to Josephus,[42] it took eight years to build the first phase of the temple and its courts, which would bring it down to 16/15 B.C., and to add forty-six years from that date would mean that Jesus was speaking to the Jews at the Passover of A.D. 30.[43]

This view is not acceptable for three reasons. First, the rebuilding of the temple, which according to Josephus' *Antiquitates Judaicae* (xv. 11. 1 § 380) began in the eighteenth year of Herod's reign, coincides with the arrival of Augustus in Syria,[44] which according to Dio Cassius occurred in the

[39]Jos. *Ant.* xx. 9. 7 § 219.
[40]Jos. *Ant.* xv. 11. 1 § 380.
[41]Jos. *BJ* i. 21. 1 § 401.
[42]Jos. *Ant.* xv. 11. 5 § 420.
[43]Thomas Corbishley, "The Chronology of the Reign of Herod the Great," *The Journal of Theological Studies*, XXXVI (January, 1935), 22-27. Jeremias also states that Josephus reckons from the two starting points but he concludes that Herod began his construction of the temple in 20/19 B.C. (Jeremias, *Jerusalem*, pp. 21-22). How Jeremias comes to this conclusion is not explained and is incomprehensible.
[44]Josephus states (*Ant.* xv. 10. 3 § 354) that Augustus arrived in Syria after Herod reigned seventeen years which would make it his eighteenth year of rule.

spring or summer of 20 B.C.[45] This is corroborated in Josephus' other account, where he states that this Augustan visit to Syria was ten years after his first visit[46] in 30 B.C. Therefore, since the eighteenth year of Herod's reign was from Nisan 1, 20 B.C. to Nisan 1, 19 B.C.,[47] Josephus must have reckoned from 37 B.C. and not 40 B.C. Second, for Corbishley to state that Josephus reckoned from two different starting points, he theorizes that Josephus had intended to compute from 37 B.C. but did not because "he mistakenly presumed that his sources did the same"[48] when in fact they reckoned from 40 B.C. This can neither be proved nor disproved. However, it seems better to say that Josephus' statement in *Bellum Judaicum* (i. 21. 1 § 401) that Herod restored the temple in his fifteenth year might be an error on the part of either Josephus or a scribe[49] or that it might refer to the time of preparation before actual construction.[50] Third, Corbishley's computation is invalid. He felt that the temple was completed by Jesus' first Passover in A.D. 30. But if one begins in 23/22 B.C. and adds eight years for its building and then adds forty-six years one does not come to A.D. 30 but A.D. 32/33. This would leave little, if any, time for Jesus' ministry.

In conclusion, the Corbishley theory is unacceptable. Rather it is best to think that Josephus reckoned Herod's eighteenth year from 37 B.C. and that the commencement of the temple reconstruction was in 20/19 B.C.

DISTINCTION OF TERMS FOR THE TEMPLE

It seems that a better approach to the problem is to determine what the Jews meant by the term "temple" when

---

[45]Dio Cassius liv. 7. 4-6. Dio states that Augustus went to Syria in the spring of the year when Marcus Apuleius and Publius Silius were consuls which was 20 B.C.
[46]Jos. *BJ* i. 20. 4 § 399.
[47]That Josephus had reckoned the regnal years of Herod the Great from Nisan 1 is discussed by Schürer, I, 326-28 n. 165.
[48]Corbishley, *The Journal of Theological Studies*, XXXVI, 26-27 n. 3.
[49]For a possible scribal error, see Finegan, pp. 277-78.
[50]Schürer, I, 292 n. 12.

they were debating with Jesus.[51] There are two Greek words for temple which are distinguished by Josephus. The first term ἱερόν refers to the whole sacred area which includes three courts or enclosures. The first court was the "Court of the Gentiles." Within it was the second court, namely, the "Court of the Women." There only Jews and their wives could enter. Gentiles were not allowed. The third court was within the second court and only Jewish men were allowed to enter it. Also within this third court there was the "Priests' Court," open only to the priests. The second term for the temple is ναός which is the sacred building alone, and it was located within the Priests' Court.[52] Both terms are translated "temple" in the English with no distinction.

The Gospels make the same distinction. For example, in referring to the whole sacred area ἱερόν is used (Matt. 21:12 = Mark 11:15 = Luke 19:45) while on the other hand ναός is used when speaking of the sacred building (Matt. 27:51 = Mark 15:38 = Luke 23:45). John's Gospel is consistent with this distinction, for notice in 2:14-15 that Jesus found the money-changers in the temple court, that is, τὸ ἱερόν (cf. also John 5:14; 7:14, 28; 8:2, 20, 59; 10:53; 11:56; 18:20) while in 2:19-20 John uses ὁ ναός when the Jews were talking about the destruction of the temple edifice. Therefore, the Jews were speaking of the temple edifice and not the whole sacred precincts.

Returning to Josephus it seems clear that the first part of Herod's rebuilding the temple was the temple edifice which was done by the priests in one year and six months.[53] Since the reconstruction began in 20/19 B.C., the sanctuary would have been completed in 18/17 B.C. Adding forty-six to the last figure brings it up to A.D. 29/30. The Jews' statement would mean that the temple edifice had stood for forty-six years.

---

[51] The present author wishes to express his appreciation for the contribution that Finegan has made with respect to the Jews' reply to Jesus in John 2:20 (Finegan, pp. 278-80).
[52] Cf. Jos. *Ant.* xv. 11. 5 §§ 417-20. This distinction is also readily seen in describing Solomon's temple, see Jos. *Ant.* viii. 3. 9 §§ 95-96.
[53] Jos. *Ant.* xv. 11. 6 § 421.

Both old and recent translations (e.g., AV, ASV, RSV, NEB, NASB, and NIV) translate it as though the building process was still continuing. Grammarians and commentators see the aorist passive οἰκοδομήθη "to build" as a constative aorist[54] noting that the process of building was for forty-six years. But Morris finds it difficult to accept the idea of a constative aorist when the building process was still going on.[55] In fact both Morris and Westcott contend that the Jews were referring to the completion of a definite stage of the work and that no building was going on when these words were spoken.[56] However, is it not better to note the distinction of the two terms for temple, and that the Jews were not talking about the temple precincts (ἱερόν) which were in the process of construction until A.D. 63, but they were referring to the temple edifice (ναός) which was completed in 18/17 B.C.? The aorist could be constative in that it took one and a half years to build the temple edifice or it could be an effective or perfective aorist in that one looks at the conclusion or results of the action, namely, the temple has stood as a completed building for forty-six years.[57] The latter view does more justice to the temporal dative, ἔτεσιν, in that the completed building extended for a forty-six year time period. Therefore, the Jews were asking Jesus how He would be able to raise up in three days the temple edifice which had stood for forty-six years.

Since the temple reconstruction began in 20/19 B.C. and the temple edifice was completed in 18/17 B.C., forty-six

---

[54]A. T. Robertson, *A Grammar of the Greek New Testament in the Light of Historical Research* (4th ed.; New York, 1923), p. 833; C. F. D. Moule, *An Idiom Book of New Testament Greek* (2nd ed.; Cambridge, 1959), p. 11; William Hendriksen, *Exposition of the Gospel according to John* (Grand Rapids, 1953), I, 125 n. 64; Leon Morris, *The Gospel according to John* (Grand Rapids, 1971), p. 200 n. 81.
[55]Morris, p. 200 n. 81.
[56]*Ibid.;* B. F. Westcott, *The Gospel according to St. John* (London, 1882), p. 43.
[57]See Corbishley, *The Journal of Theological Studies,* XXXVI, 26; Finegan, pp. 279-80; E. Power, "John 2, 20 and the Date of the Crucifixion," *Biblica,* IX (July, 1928), 268-77; cf. also Robertson, pp. 834-35, 840-41; Nigel Turner, *Syntax,* Vol. III of *A Grammar of New Testament Greek* (Edinburgh, 1963), p. 72; Moule, pp. 11, 13.

years later would bring the date to the year A.D. 29/30. This means, then, that Jesus' first Passover was the spring of A.D. 30. The Jews were telling Jesus that the temple edifice had stood for forty-six years and was now just beginning its forty-seventh year. This fits well with the results of the first part of this chapter where it was concluded that Jesus was baptized in the summer or autumn of A.D. 29. Thus there was a period of anywhere from four to nine months between Christ's baptism and the first Passover in His ministry.

"NOT YET FIFTY YEARS OLD"

In John 8:57 the Jews said to Jesus, "You are not yet fifty years old." Irenaeus held that Jesus was in His forties, for if Jesus were in His thirties they would have said, "You are not yet forty years old."[58] Ogg takes this chronological note in John 8:57 seriously and doubts that Luke 3:23 can serve any chronological purpose.[59] But certainly the opposite is more likely. Luke 3:23 is a precise statement whereas John 8:57 indicates that the Jews were emphasizing Jesus' youth in contrast to His claim that He existed before Abraham. Therefore, John 8:57 is not helpful in trying to establish the commencement of Christ's ministry.

SUMMARY AND CONCLUSION

Luke gives specific chronological notes for the commencement of Christ's public ministry. In 3:1-2 the evangelist first gives the fifteenth year of Tiberius as the time when John the Baptist's ministry began. Since Luke was writing to a Roman official, it was concluded that he reckoned from either the Julian Calendar or Tiberius' regnal year. Both of these methods were used by Roman historians. Therefore, it was concluded that Luke's reference to the fifteenth year of Tiberius points to the year A.D. 29 as the

---

[58]Irenaeus *Adversus Haereses* ii. 22. 6.
[59]G. Ogg, "Chronology of the New Testament," *Peake's Commentary on the Bible,* ed. by Matthew Black (London, 1962), p. 728.

year for the commencement of the Baptist's ministry and that Christ's ministry began shortly thereafter.

In the same chapter Luke adds another chronological notice. He states that Christ was "about thirty years of age" when He began His ministry. Since the phrase "about thirty years of age" is an elastic expression, it was concluded that it allows for a flexibility of two or three years. If John's ministry began in the early part of A.D. 29 and Jesus was baptized in the summer or autumn of that same year, He would have been only thirty-two years of age at the commencement of His ministry. Therefore, both Luke 3:1-2 and 23 point to A.D. 29 as the year that Christ began His public ministry.

The evidence in John 2:20 also supports the A.D. 29 date. In the first Passover of Jesus' public ministry, Jesus stated that He could destroy the temple edifice and raise it up in three days. The Jews asked how He could destroy and rebuild in three days a structure which had stood for forty-six years. Since the reconstruction of the temple edifice was completed in 18/17 B.C., the addition of forty-six years makes the date of the conversation recorded in John 2:20 the Passover of A.D. 30. Therefore, the first Passover of Jesus' public ministry followed by four to nine months the beginning of His public ministry.

The picture given in the Gospels is in line with the chronological outline given above. After John baptized Jesus, there was the temptation (Matt 4:1-11; Mark 1:12-13; Luke 4:1-13); the call of His first disciples (John 1:35-51); the wedding feast at Cana of Galilee (John 2:1-11); His journey to Capernaum (John 2:12); and then His journey to Jerusalem to attend the first Passover of His ministry on Nisan 14, or April 7, A.D. 30.[60]

Therefore, it is concluded that Christ's ministry began sometime in the summer or autumn of A.D. 29.

[60]Parker and Dubberstein, p. 46.

Chapter III

The Duration of Christ's Ministry

Since the gospel writers never specifically state the duration of Christ's public ministry, there have been differences of interpretation regarding the sequences and duration of His ministry. Having concluded in the previous chapter that Jesus' public ministry began in the summer or autumn of A.D. 29, the next logical step is to determine the duration of His ministry. In attempting to answer this question, widely ranging theories have been offered. The more extreme views will be considered first.

EXTREME VIEWS UNACCEPTABLE

Scholars have calculated its duration from three or four months[1] to sometime between ten and twenty years.[2] To have a ministry for only three to six months, one needs to compress the ministry unmercifully. If one accepts the chronological notes in the Gospels with any seriousness the ministry of Christ is surely longer than a few months. On the other hand in Irenaeus' attempt to refute Valentinus' view of a one-year ministry of Jesus, he states, though not clearly, that since Jesus began His ministry when He was "about thirty years of age" (Luke 3:23), His ministry continued into His forties since the Jews in John 8:57 state that Christ was not yet fifty years old. This makes the ministry of Jesus somewhere between ten and twenty years long. But the

---

[1]Ch. Guigneburt, *Jesus,* trans. by S. H. Hooke (London, 1935), p. 211. For a ministry of four to seven months, see Hans Windisch, "Die Dauer der öffentlichen Wirksamkeit Jesu nach den vier Evangelisten," *Zeitschrift für die neutestamentliche Wissenschaft,* XII (1911), 141-75.
[2]Irenaeus *Adversus Haereses* ii. 22. 5-6.

statement in John 8:57 is not a precise chronological note. Rather it indicates that the Jews were emphasizing Jesus' youth in contrast to His claim that He existed before Abraham. A ten- to twenty-year ministry would not fit into the framework of the Gospels, namely, if Jesus' ministry started in A.D. 29, He was crucified before Pilate's departure from Judea in the winter of A.D. 36/37. Thus neither of these two extreme views are acceptable when held up to the light of Scripture.

ALTERNATIVE SOLUTIONS CONSIDERED

Various theories from one to four years have been proposed for the length of our Lord's ministry. The order of their discussion will be as follows: one-year, two-year, four-year, and finally the three-year ministry. Each theory will be presented in a two-part format. An opening statement of the view will provide a brief explanation, and the critque of the view will offer analysis and evaluation. First, then, the one-year theory.

ONE-YEAR THEORY

Statement of the view. Early Gnostic commentators such as Valentinus (who was born *ca.* A.D. 100, educated at Alexandria, and later taught at Rome) thought that the duration of Jesus' ministry was about a year because of Luke 4:19 where it quotes Isaiah 61:2: "To proclaim the acceptable year of the Lord." However, Valentinus' contemporary, Irenaeus, from whom one obtains information about Valentinus, refuted this theory by indicating the number of Passovers in the Gospel of John.[3] The one-year theory was also adopted by Clement of Alexandria (*ca.* 150-215)[4] and Origen (*ca.* 185-254)[5] among others. More recent exponents of the one-year ministry of Christ are

[3]*Ibid.*
[4]Clement of Alexandria *Stromata* i. 21. 146.
[5]Origen *De Principiis* iv. 1. 5.

Belser,[6] von Soden,[7] Klausner,[8] Goguel,[9] Olmstead,[10] and probably Conzelmann.[11] These later advocates basically think that one can fit Christ's ministry in the year, beginning with His disciples' plucking the grain on the Sabbath in Mark 2:23 (fully ripened grain between Passover and Pentecost) and ending with the Passover (the only one mentioned in the Synoptic Gospels) in Mark 14:1.

Critique of the view. First, to build a one-year ministry on Luke 4:19, "To proclaim the acceptable year of the Lord," is unacceptable. The Old Testament passage was quoted to indicate that the predicted Messiah had arrived and not to indicate the duration of His ministry (this view is not held by the modern exponents of a one-year ministry of Christ).

Second, to compress a ministry of one year between Mark 2:23 and 14:1 is unlikely for two reasons. For one thing, the Gospel of John makes shipwreck of this theory since there are at least three Passovers during the ministry of Jesus: John 2:13 (Jesus' first journey to Jerusalem); 6:4 (feeding of the 5,000); and 11:55 (the passion Passover). However, Origen found no difficulty with John's Gospel because apparently his text omitted at least the words τὸ πάσχα ("the Passover") if not the whole verse of John 6:4. This left a Passover at the beginning and end of Christ's one-year ministry. Although some conjecture that Origen may have

[6]Johannes Belser, "Zur Hypothese von der einjährigen Wirksamkeit Jesu," *Biblische Zeitschrift*, I (1903), 55-63, 160-74; Johannes Belser, "Zu der Perikope von der Speisung der Fünftausend," *Biblische Zeitschrift*, II (1904), 154-76.
[7]Hermann von Soden, "Chronology," *Encyclopaedia Biblica*, ed. by T. K. Cheyne and T. Sutherland Black, I (1899), 802-3.
[8]Joseph Klausner, *Jesus of Nazareth*, trans. by Herbert Danby (London, 1925), p. 259.
[9]Maurice Goguel, *The Life of Jesus*, trans. by Olive Wyon (London, 1933), pp. 233-52.
[10]A. T. Olmstead, "The Chronology of Jesus' Life," *Anglican Theological Review*, XXIV (January, 1942), 1-26, esp. 6-11; A. T. Olmstead, *Jesus in the Light of History* (New York, 1942), p. 281.
[11]Hans Conzelmann, *History of Primitive Christianity*, trans. by John E. Steely (Nashville, 1973), p. 30.

thought the feast mentioned in 6:4[12] was the Feast of Tabernacles (since the next chapter is about the Feast of Tabernacles), it is not a tenable solution since in the context of the feast John states that there was "much grass" (6:10), indicating the celebration was in the spring rather than the autumn. Furthermore, there is no textual evidence outside of Origen for its omission. Thus, from John's Gospel there are three Passovers mentioned specifically — requiring at least a ministry of two years. The second reason for the untenability of compressing a year's ministry between Mark 2:23 and 14:1 is seen right in Mark's Gospel. In Mark 2:23 Jesus' disciples pluck the fully ripened grain and in 6:39 (feeding of the 5,000) there is the mention of "green grass" indicating another year had elapsed since 2:23. There would have been yet another year between 6:39 and the passion Passover of 14:1.

Therefore, from both John and the Synoptics it is highly untenable to hold that Jesus' ministry lasted only one year. It was at least two years.

TWO-YEAR THEORY

Statement of the view. Since the Gospel of John specifically mentions three Passovers (2:13; 6:4; 11:55), it is thought that Jesus' ministry lasted a little over two years. Early supporters for this theory are Apollinaris, bishop of Laodicea in Syria (*ca.* 310-390)[13] and Epiphanius, bishop of Salamis in Cyprus (*ca.* 315-403).[14] The most well-known recent defender of this view is Sutcliffe[15] and it is accepted

---

[12]For a discussion of this, see Brooke Foss Westcott and Fenton John Anthony Hort, *The New Testament in the Original Greek: Introduction, Appendix* (Cambridge and London, 1882), pp. 77-81. Only Hort signed the article, seemingly persuaded of the validity of the omission of "the Passover."

[13]Preserved by Jerome *Commentariorum in Danielem* ix, 24 (690).

[14]Epiphanius *Panarion* li. 30.

[15]Edmund F. Sutcliffe, *A Two Year Public Ministry Defended* (London, 1938).

by Blinzler,[16] Caird,[17] Ruckstuhl,[18] Schnackenburg,[19] Bruce,[20] and Duncan.[21]

Critique of the view. To hold to a two-year ministry, there must be a transposition of chapters 5 and 6 of the Gospel of John. There has been a great amount of discussion on the rearrangement of these chapters. Both those who rearrange the material of John's Gospel on a large scale, such as Bernard[22] and Bultmann,[23] and those who do little in rearranging of John's Gospel, such as Schnackenburg,[24] reverse the order of John 5 and 6. Since a discussion on the rearrangement of the materials in John's Gospel is beyond the scope of this chapter, only a brief statement can be made.

It is thought that it makes better geographical sense when chapters 5 and 6 are transposed, for at the end of John 4 Jesus is in Cana of Galilee, in chapter 6 He is by the Sea of Galilee, then in chapter 5 He goes up to Jerusalem, and finally in chapter 7 Jesus can no longer travel in Judea so He traveled in Galilee. It is thought, then, that the Feast of John 5:1 is the Passover mentioned in 6:4.

However, the theory of dislocations has not solved all the problems. First, and foremost, there is no textual evidence whatsoever for any other order than the traditional

[16]Josef Blinzler, *The Trial of Jesus,* trans. by Isabel and Florence McHugh (2nd ed.; Westminster, MD, 1959), pp. 74-75.
[17]George B. Caird, "The Chronology of the NT," *The Interpreter's Dictionary of the Bible,* ed. by George Arthur Buttrick, *et al.,* I (1962), 601-2.
[18]Eugen Ruckstuhl, *Chronology of the Last Days of Jesus,* trans. by Victor J. Drapela (New York, 1965), p. 6.
[19]Rudolf Schnackenburg, *The Gospel according to St. John,* trans. by Kevin Smyth (New York, 1968), I, 345.
[20]F. F. Bruce, *New Testament History* (London, 1969), p. 190.
[21]George B. Duncan, "Chronology," *The Interpreter's One-Volume Commentary on the Bible,* ed. by Charles M. Laymon (Nashville, 1971), p. 1281.
[22]J. H. Bernard, *A Critical Commentary on the Gospel according to St. John,* ed. by A. H. McNeile (Edinburgh, 1928), I, xvi-xxxiii.
[23]Rudolf Bultmann, *The Gospel of John,* trans. by G. R. Beasley-Murray, R. W. N. Hoare, and J. K. Riches (Philadelphia, 1971), pp. xiii, 111-12.
[24]Schnackenburg, I, 46.

one.[25] Second, the transposition is not really an improvement. For example, theologically Dodd thinks that in John 5:19-47 Christ is established as the divine Son which serves as a basis for Christ's claims made in chapter 6.[26] Another example is that there is no improvement in the geographical progression, for it seems from John 7:3 that Jesus had not recently been in Jerusalem performing miracles, which is strange if chapter 7 follows immediately after chapter 5.[27] Other examples could be given but suffice it to say with Smith that the theories of transposition are not compelling and that "the burden of proof in this matter is upon the one whoever rearranges the text, and he must not only show that this order is preferable but also that the present one is so exceedingly difficult as to be virtually impossible."[28] Therefore, although a transposition is possible there is no overwhelming evidence for it. Hence, accepting that John 5-7 are in proper order, the two-year ministry of Christ goes out the window. It is not good to base a theory of a two-year ministry on the supposition that there must be a transposition of John 5 and 6 for which there is no manuscript evidence nor any other compelling reason for the transposition. Hence, there is a need for Christ's ministry to have been longer than two years.

FOUR-YEAR THEORY

Statement of the view. Stauffer and Cheney think that Jesus had a ministry of a little over four years. Each writer

---

[25]Cf. Leon Morris, *The Gospel according to John* (Grand Rapids, 1971), p. 297; Raymond E. Brown, *The Gospel according to John* (Garden City, NY, 1966), I, 236; C. K. Barrett, *The Gospel according to St. John* (London, 1956), pp. 19-20, 209, 227.
[26]C. H. Dodd, *The Interpretation of the Fourth Gospel* (Cambridge, 1954), p. 340.
[27]Brown, I, 235.
[28]Dwight Moody Smith, Jr., *The Composition and Order of the Fourth Gospel* (New Haven, 1965), p. 130; see also pp. 128-34; cf. also Howard M. Teeple, "Methodology in Source Analysis of the Fourth Gospel," *Journal of Biblical Literature*, LXXXI (September, 1962), 279-86; Werner Georg Kümmel, *Introduction to the New Testament*, trans. by Howard Clark Kee (17th rev. ed.; Nashville, 1975), pp. 204-6.

bases his theory of a four-year ministry on different evidence.

Stauffer has summarized his view well when he writes:

> The fourth gospel, on the other hand, deals with a period of about four years (between five Passover feasts) in which the arrest of the Baptist lies midway. In John 1.29, 41 ff., the season of the Passover is presumed. In John 2.13, 23 we hear of the second Passover. In John 3.24 the Baptist is still at work. In 4.35 it is winter time. The third Passover is not mentioned. In John 5.1 it is autumn, the feast of Tabernacles. In John 5.35 the Baptist is no longer active. In John 6.4 the fourth Passover is at hand. In John 7.2 it is autumn once again; in John 10.22 winter again, the feast of the Dedication of the temple. In John 11.55 we hear of the fifth Passover feast, the Passover of death.[29]

Cheney feels that one great problem with a three-year ministry is that "it compresses too many events into the last six months of His ministry."[30] It is felt that Jesus' departure from Galilee to go to Jerusalem for the Feast of Tabernacles in John 7 cannot be the same departure as given in Luke 9:51. Therefore, one needs a four-year ministry. Cheney's reconstruction would be as follows: the first Passover is recorded in John 2:13; the feast in 5:1 is the Feast of Tabernacles; the second Passover is alluded to in Luke 6:1; the third Passover is in John 6:4; the fourth Passover is alluded to in the story of the temple tax in Matthew 17:24 and the time when Pilate mingled the blood of the Galileans with the sacrifices in Luke 13:1; and the fifth and final Passover is mentioned in John 11:55. Cheney then concludes by stating that the parable of the barren fig tree (Luke 13:6-9) substantiates a four-year ministry.[31]

In conclusion Stauffer adds a Passover before the one mentioned in John 2:13 and another Passover between the ones mentioned in John 2:13 and 6:4, whereas Cheney adds a

[29]Ethelbert Stauffer, *Jesus and His Story*, trans. by Dorothea M. Barton (London, 1960), p. 17.
[30]Johnston M. Cheney, *The Life of Christ in Stereo*, ed. by Stanley A. Ellisen (Portland, OR, 1969), p. 227.
[31]*Ibid.*, pp. 229-36.

Passover between John 2:13 and 6:4 and another one between John 6:4 and 11:55.

Critique of the view. First, Stauffer has to presume that
Jesus went to Jerusalem for a Passover right after He had
been baptized by John and when certain disciples began to
follow Him (John 1:29-51).[32] But this is a big presumption for
there is no indication whatever from the text of John that this
was a Passover season nor that any journey to Jerusalem was
made. In fact the text states that Jesus came to John, who was
in Bethany beyond the Jordan (John 1:28-29), and three days
later Jesus intended to go to Galilee (1:43). Furthermore, the
next geographical notation given by John is Christ's attend-
ance at the wedding in Cana of Galilee (2:1). If one accepts
Stauffer's view then one has to squeeze one whole year
between John 1:51 and 2:13 — for according to Stauffer 2:13
is Jesus' second Passover. However, there is no indication in
John 1:29-51 that Jesus celebrated a Passover in Jerusalem.

Second, Cheney thinks that Jesus' first Passover is
recorded in John 2:13, and, that Jesus' second Passover is
alluded to in Luke 6:1.[33] When one looks at the setting of this
story of the disciples plucking the grain, it is evident that it
was the springtime. He feels that this event must fit between
the first and the third Passover. This is reasonable for John's
first explicit mention of a Passover is in 2:13, which is very
early in Jesus' ministry, and the next explicit reference of a
Passover is in 6:4, which is in the context of the feeding of the
5,000 (quite a bit later in Jesus' ministry, as is seen also
in the Synoptics: Matt. 14:13-21; Mark 6:32-44; Luke
9:10-17).[34] The third Passover is the one mentioned in John
6:4 and the fourth Passover is not explicitly mentioned in
John but it is between the Passovers mentioned in John 6:4
and 11:55. Cheney thinks that one cannot identify Jesus'
departure from Galilee to attend the Feast of Tabernacles in

[32]Stauffer, pp. 17, 59.
[33]Cheney, pp. 229-30.
[34]Cheney attempts to demonstrate that Luke 6:1 is referring to the second

John 7:2 with that of Luke 9:51 because John 7:2 indicates that Jesus went directly to Jerusalem whereas Jesus' departure in Luke 9:51 involved several months journey before reaching Jerusalem.[35] Another unsatisfactory solution according to Cheney is to fit Luke 9:51 — 19:28 after the Feast of Dedication (John 10:22-42) and before the resurrection of Lazarus (John 11:1-53) because this would mean all of the ministry of Christ in Luke 9:51 — 19:28 would need to be fitted into a two-month period.[36] So he suggests that one allow for another year's ministry between John 10 and 11 similar to those who hold a three-year ministry have a year lapse between John 5 and 6. This is further substantiated from the Synoptics, for the annual temple tax (Matt. 17:24) and the massacre of the Galileans (Luke 13:1) would fit within the extra Passover between chapters 10 and 11 of John's Gospel.[37]

However, Cheney's solution is not satisfactory. First, the insertion of a year between John 10 and 11 is based entirely upon an argument of silence. An additional year is allowed between the explicitly mentioned Passovers in John 2:13 and 6:4 because there is internal evidence within John's Gospel (which will be discussed below). But there is no internal evidence in the Gospel of John for an additional year between John 10 and 11.

Passover of Jesus' ministry by accepting the debatable reading of δευτεροπρώτῳ (the "second first" Sabbath) and states that this has reference to the second of the seven Sabbaths between Passover and Pentecost. But this is dubious for not only is the textual reading highly questionable but also even if one accepts the reading, there are many different interpretations as to its meaning and so one cannot say that it pinpoints the occasion of the second Passover (Cheney, pp. 229-30; for different interpretations, see F. Godet, *A Commentary on the Gospel of St. Luke*, trans. by E. W. Shalders and M. D. Cusin [Edinburgh, n.d.], I, 284-86; Alfred Plummer, *A Critical and Exegetical Commentary on the Gospel according to S. Luke* [4th ed.; Edinburgh, 1905], pp. 165-66). To hold to a view that is based on a questionable interpretation which in turn is built upon a questionable textual reading is immediately suspect.

[35]Cheney, pp. 227, 231-33.

[36]*Ibid.*, p. 227.

[37]*Ibid.*, pp. 233-34.

Second, the Synoptic parallels can be dated satisfactorily without an extra year between John 10 and 11. Although the temple tax was normally collected in Adar (the month before Passover),[38] there is reason to believe from Matthew 17:24-27 that these collectors of the temple tax came after the due-date. The text indicates that Jesus and His disciples had just arrived in Capernaum and thus they were away from their hometown when the collection was normally made.[39] It seems that Christ was probably in Capernaum (Matt. 15:1-20) just before He went to Tyre and Sidon and after which there were some miracles, the journey to Caesarea Philippi followed by the transfiguration, after which He returned to Capernaum (Matt. 17:24). Hence, Christ and His disciples had been away for some time and would have missed the temple tax collectors. Regarding the massacre of the Galileans (Luke 13:1), it could well fit into the Passover mentioned in John 6:4.[40]

Third, although many efforts have been made to attempt to fit the central section of Luke 9:51 — 19:28 with John's Gospel, a plausible solution is given by Wieseler.[41] He points out that John mentions three journeys, namely, the Feast of Tabernacles (7:2), to Bethany for raising Lazarus (11:7, 17-18), and the final Passover (11:55). Luke likewise in the central section of his book speaks of going to Jerusalem three times (9:51; 13:22; 17:11). It is highly possible that the three journeys mentioned in these two Gospels correspond. Therefore, there is no need to add an additional year between John 10 and 11. Although there are many events to be placed within a seven-month period, it is not unreasonable.

[38]Mishnah: Shekalim i. 1-3.
[39]See Alfred Edersheim, *The Life and Times of Jesus the Messiah* (3rd ed.; London, 1886), II, 112-13.
[40]Josef Blinzler, "Eine Bemerkung zum Geschichtsrahmen des Johannesevangeliums," *Biblica*, XXXVI (1955), 20-35.
[41]Karl Wieseler, *Chronologische Synopse der vier Evangelium* (Hamburg, 1843), pp. 316-32; cf. also C. J. Ellicott, *Historical Lectures on the Life of Our Lord Jesus Christ* (London, 1861), pp. 236-77; Edersheim, II, 126-27; A. T. Robertson, *A Harmony of the Gospels for Students of the Life of Christ* (New York, 1922), pp. 278-79.

In conclusion, then, both theories espousing a four-year ministry do not offer convincing evidence. One of the most obvious weaknesses is that both theories add an extra year to the Gospel of John — an addition for which there is no evidence from within the Gospel itself. Other questions and difficulties result as well when one year is added to John's Gospel. The discussion now turns to the last of the four theories, the three-year ministry of Christ.

THREE-YEAR THEORY

Statement of the view. It is thought that besides the three Passovers explicitly mentioned in the Gospel of John (2:13; 6:4; 11:55), there was an additional year of the Lord's ministry between the Passovers mentioned in 2:13 and 6:4. There is in this view no need for transposition of John 5 and 6 as is required by the two-year theory.

Early advocates of this theory are Melito of Sardis (d. *ca*. 190)[42] and Eusebius (*ca*. 260-340)[43] among many others.[44] The most well-known defender of the three-year ministry of Christ is Ogg[45] and it is also held by such men as Robertson,[46] Armstrong,[47] Hendriksen,[48] Madison,[49] and Guthrie.[50]

Critique of the view. One problem with an addition of a year between the Passovers of John 2:13 and 6:4 is that there

[42]Preserved in Anastasius Sinaita *Viae Dux* xiii (115).
[43]Eusebius *Chronica*, ed. by Rudolf Helm, Vol. XXIV of *Die griechischen christlichen Schriftsteller* (Leipzig, 1913), pp. 173-74; *Demonstratio Evangelica* viii. 2. 93-111; *Historia Ecclesiasticus* i. 10. 3-4.
[44]See a good discussion by George Ogg, *The Chronology of the Public Ministry of Jesus* (Cambridge, 1940), pp. 76-90, 98-103, 119-28.
[45]*Ibid*., pp. 1-149.
[46]Robertson, pp. 267-70.
[47]William P. Armstrong, "Chronology of the New Testament," *The International Standard Bible Encyclopaedia*, ed. by James Orr, *et al*., I (1929), 647.
[48]William Hendriksen, *Exposition of the Gospel according to John* (Grand Rapids, 1953), I, 187-89.
[49]Leslie P. Madison, "Problems of Chronology in the Life of Christ" (unpublished Th.D. dissertation, Dallas Theological Seminary, 1963), pp. 102-48.
[50]Donald Guthrie, *New Testament Introduction* (3rd ed.; Downers Grove, IL, 1970), pp. 294-95.

is no mention of an additional Passover by John. This is an argument from silence but not all the feasts are mentioned in John, for example the Feast of Pentecost. Also, the Synoptic accounts require another year between the Passovers of 2:13 and 6:4. One point of chronology that is common to all four Gospels is the feeding of the 5,000 (Matt. 14:13-21; Mark 6:32-44; Luke 9:10-17; John 6:1-15) which is dated sometime near the Passover of John 6:4. Confirmation of this is given in Mark 6:39 where there is the incidental mention that the grass was green — indicating the springtime, the time of the Passover. But earlier in the Synoptic Gospels there is recorded the incident of the disciples plucking grain (Matt. 12:1; Mark 2:23; Luke 6:1) which would point to the harvest season a year earlier. On the other hand the Passover of John 2:13 is too early for the incident of the disciples plucking grain for John 2:13 occurred shortly after He had been baptized and had started His ministry. Also, after the Passover of John 2:13 His ministry was in Judea whereas the plucking of the grain occurred after He had been in Galilee. So the plucking of the grain would fit well around the time of the Passover between the Passovers mentioned in John 2:13 and 6:4.

There are also within the Gospel of John two notes of time that would indicate there was an additional year between the Passovers of John 2:13 and 6:4. The first note of time is John 4:35: "Do you not say, 'There are yet four months and (then) the harvest?'" Some commentators take this as a proverb indicating the time interval between sowing and harvesting was a four-month period and thus it has no historical value indicating a particular time of the year when Jesus uttered these words.[51] Further, it is thought by those holding this view that from the context one sees Jesus' request for water pointing to a time of heat and four months

---

[51]E.g., Bernard, I, 155-57; Barrett, p. 202; C. H. Dodd, *Historical Tradition in the Fourth Gospel* (Cambridge, 1963), p. 394; Brown, I, 174; Morris, pp. 278-79; Barnabas Lindars, *The Gospel of John* (London, 1972), p. 195.

before harvest would be during January/February when plenty of surface water was available. However, there are certain indications that Jesus was not giving a proverb but was referring to the actual time of the year. They are: (1) there is no attestation of the existence of such a proverb;[52] (2) the adverb ἔτι "yet" "would not suit a proverb; the words: since the sowing, would have been necessary;"[53] and (3) it is not a period of four months but six months between the sowing and harvesting in Palestine, since wheat sowing begins in October/November[54] and is harvested in April/May.[55] On the basis of these arguments[56] it is reasonable to conclude that this statement arose out of the circumstances at the time it was spoken and therefore it is to be recognized as a note of time. This would place Jesus in Samaria in January/February after the Passover of John 2:13. The objection is raised that this incident cannot be in the winter but at a time when it was hot and there was a lack of water. But there is no indication from the text that it was hot but only that Jesus wanted water because He was weary, and being in the city of Sychar there would not be available surface water — one would need to get it from the well. Furthermore, even if there was surface water it may not have been fit to drink. He also may have wanted water from the well in order to talk to the woman who opened up His ministry in Samaria. In conclusion, then, it is reasonable to

[52]Even Bultmann (p. 196 n. 4) admits this.
[53]Frederick Louis Godet, *Commentary on the Gospel of John,* trans. by Timothy Dwight (3rd ed.; New York, 1886), I, 435. Hendriksen (p. 173) states: "In a *proverb* one would expect simply: 'There are four months between seedtime and harvest,' or simply: 'There are four months; then comes the harvest,' but not, 'There are yet four months; then comes the harvest.' " Cf. also Wieseler, pp. 214-17.
[54]The latest date for sowing according to the Mishnah (Taanith i. 7) is Marheshwan 17th (October/November).
[55]Gustaf Dalman, *Arbeit und Sitte in Palästina* (Gütersloh, 1928), I, 164-67, 413-18; cf. also Hermann L. Strack and Paul Billerbeck, *Kommentar zum Neuen Testament aus Talmud und Midrasch* (München, 1924), II, 439-40.
[56]For further argumentation and refutation of other theories, see Ogg, pp. 29-41.

accept John 4 :35 as a historical note which indicates that Jesus was in Samaria some time after the Passover of 2:13, 23.

The second note of time is in John 5:1 where it states: "After these things there was a feast of the Jews, and Jesus went up to Jerusalem." There are several problems that need to be mentioned before looking at its chronological contributions. First, although there is some good textual evidence for an article before "feast" (which probably would point to one of the three pilgrim feasts), it seems that there is better support for the omission of the article. Second, to identify this feast with certainty is impossible. In attempting to identify this feast various scholars have suggested Purim (March),[57] Passover (March/April),[58] Pentecost (May/June),[59] Wood-offering (August),[60] Trumpets (September/October),[61] Day of Atonement (October),[62] and Tabernacles (October).[63] Of these listed the most improbable time would be the Day of Atonement because it is hardly "a festival."[64] The Feast of Purim does not fit the character of Jesus' discourse in John 5[65] and it is unlikely that Jesus would have attended a feast which was purely boisterous merriment in character.[66] Since the Feast of

---

[57]E.g., Wieseler, pp. 205-23; Godet, *John,* I, 452-54.

[58]E.g., preferred by Robertson, pp. 42 n. *, 270; Hendriksen, p. 188. Of course, many of those who accept the transposition of John 5 and 6 would see the feast of 5:1 as the Passover referring back to John 6:4 (e.g., Barnard, I, 225; Bultmann, p. 240).

[59]John Calvin, *The Gospel according to St. John,* trans. by T. H. L. Parker (Grand Rapids, 1959), IV, pt. 1, p. 116; John Albert Bengel, *Gnomon of the New Testament,* trans. by Andrew R. Fausset, *et al.* (2nd ed.; Edinburgh, 1859), II, 302.

[60]Edersheim, I, 423; II, 768-69.

[61]B. F. Westcott, *The Gospel according to St. John* (London, 1882), pp. 92-94.

[62]C.E. Caspari, *A Chronological and Geographical Introduction to the Life of Christ,* trans. by Maurice J. Evans (Edinburgh, 1876), pp. 130-32.

[63]Ogg, pp. 298-300, 322-23; Stauffer, pp. 17, 18, 66, 165 n. 7, 173 n. 16; Jack Finegan, *Handbook of Biblical Chronology* (Princeton, 1964), pp. 283-84.

[64]Westcott, p. 93.

[65]*Ibid.*

[66]Edersheim, I, 768.

Wood-offering was of such insignificance and Trumpets was little attended by the Jews, it is unlikely that Jesus would have attended them.

This leaves the three pilgrim feasts which the Jewish males were required to attend (Exod. 23:14-17; 34:23; Deut. 16:16), namely, Passover, Pentecost, and Tabernacles. To decide which of these three feasts is meant is difficult indeed. The present author, with great hesitation, prefers the Feast of Tabernacles for the following reasons. First, the Feast of Tabernacles is elsewhere referred to in John simply as "the feast"[67] (7:2, 10, 14, 37) whereas the Passover is not referred to as "the feast" but rather "the Passover" (2:13, 23; 6:4; 11:55 *bis;* 12:1; 13:1; 18:39; 19:14). Second, although various conjectures have been given for various feasts, it seems that the Feast of Tabernacles fits better chronologically in the Gospel of John. In John 2:13 there is the first Passover. Then in 4:35 there is the reference to January/February after the first Passover. If 5:1 were the next Passover, it would come immediately after 4:35 whereas there is a hint of some extended time between 4:35 and 5:1 before going back to Jerusalem. The next chronological note is the Passover of 6:4, which is followed by the Feast of Tabernacles in 7:2, making 7:2 a year from the conjectured Feast of Tabernacles in 5:1.

In conclusion then, it seems that any of the three pilgrim feasts is more viable than the lesser feasts, and of the three pilgrim feasts, the Feast of Tabernacles probably has a slight edge. Thus Blinzler's contention that in order to hold to a three-year ministry the feast of John 5:1 must be a Passover[68] is false. It has been shown that many advocates of a three-year ministry identify the Feast of John 5:1 with Jewish feasts other than Passover.

CONCLUSION

The one-year theory for the duration of Christ's ministry is not at all plausible if one takes the Gospel of John seri-

---

[67]If one accepts the article before the word "feast" in John 5:1, this argument gains strength.
[68]Blinzler, *The Trial of Jesus*, p. 74.

ously. The two-year view is based upon the transposition of John 5 and 6 for which there is no textual or any other evidence. The four-year theory is built upon suppositions for which there is no evidence. The three-year ministry has good bases from both the Synoptics and the Gospel of John. Therefore the three-year ministry of Jesus from the first Passover to the passion Passover is the most viable option. Of course, since Jesus' baptism and public ministry preceded the first Passover, the total length of His ministry would be about three and a half years.

OUTLINE OF CHRIST'S MINISTRY

Because of the scope of these chapters only a brief outline of Christ's ministry can be given. Of course, there is debate on some of the points, but such discussion goes beyond our purpose here.

MINISTRY BEFORE THE FIRST PASSOVER

It was concluded in the previous chapter that Jesus' public ministry began in the summer or autumn of A.D. 29. After John baptized Jesus, there was the temptation (Matt. 4:1-11; Mark 1:12-13; Luke 4:1-13); the call of His first disciples (John 1:35-51); the wedding feast at Cana of Galilee (John 2:1-11); His journey to Capernaum (John 2:12); and then His journey to Jerusalem to attend the first Passover of His ministry (John 2:13, 23) on Nisan 14, or April 7, A.D. 30.[69]

MINISTRY FROM PASSOVER OF 30 TO PASSOVER OF 31

After the Passover of A.D. 30, Jesus' ministry was primarily in Jerusalem (John 3:1-21) and Judea (3:22-36). With the imprisonment of John the Baptist, Jesus then moved from Judea to go to Galilee (Matt. 4:12; Mark 1:14; Luke 4:14; John 4:3). He passed through Samaria and ministered there (John 4:4-42) around January/February of A.D.

---

[69]Richard A. Parker and Waldo H. Dubberstein, *Babylonian Chronology 626 B.C.—A.D. 75* (2nd ed.; Providence, 1956), p. 46.

31 (4:35). He then moved into Galilee and ministered there (Matt. 4:13-17; Mark 1:14-15; Luke 4:14-15; John 4:43-46).

MINISTRY FROM PASSOVER OF 31 TO PASSOVER OF 32

The plucking of grain on the Sabbath (Mark 2:23-28; Luke 6:1-5; cf. Matt. 12:1-8) would have been around the time of the second Passover of Jesus' ministry. There is the continuation of the Galilean ministry including the Sermon on the Mount and the extensive healing ministry. It may well be around the summer of 31 that Jesus was rejected by the religious leaders who attributed His ministry to Beelzebub (Matt. 12:22-37; Mark 3:19-30) after which He spoke in parables. If one accepts the feast of John 5:1 as being the Feast of Tabernacles, Jesus would have been in Jerusalem for the feast during October 21-28, A.D. 31.[70] Returning to Galilee Jesus sent out the twelve (Mark 6:6-13; Luke 9:1-6), received the news of the beheading of John the Baptist, the twelve returned, after which He withdrew with the twelve. This is followed by the feeding of the 5,000 (Matt. 14:13-21; Mark 6:32-44; Luke 9:10-17; John 6:1-15) around the Passover (John 6:4) of A.D. 32, which would have been April 13/14.[71]

MINISTRY FROM PASSOVER OF 32 TO PASSOVER OF 33

From the Passover to the Feast of Tabernacles of 32 was a period of Jesus' retirement from public ministry.[72] Shortly after the feeding of the 5,000 Jesus and His disciples withdrew to Phoenicia (Matt. 15:21-28; Mark 7:24-30). They returned via the Decapolis. This was followed by the feeding of the 4,000 (Matt. 15:32-39; Mark 8:1-10), the great confession at Caesarea-Philippi (Matt. 16:13-20; Mark 8:27-30; Luke 9:18-21), and the transfiguration (Matt. 17:1-9; Mark 9:2-10; Luke 9:28-36) as well as ministries of teaching and healing.

[70]*Ibid.*
[71]*Ibid.*
[72]For more discussion on this, see Harold W. Hoehner, *Herod Antipas* (Cambridge, 1972), pp. 317-30.

John states that Jesus went up to Jerusalem to the Feast of Tabernacles (7:2, 10) which would have been September 10-17, A.D. 32.[73] All three Synoptic Gospels state that Jesus went up to Jerusalem (Matt. 19:1; Mark 10:1; Luke 9:51). The real question is whether or not one can fit Luke's central section (9:51 — 19:28) with the Gospel of John. Wieseler has suggested that the three journeys mentioned in John (7:2; 11:7, 17-18; 11:55) correspond to the three journeys to Jerusalem in Luke's central section (9:51; 13:22; 17:11).[74] The present writer follows this scheme with slight modifications.

The first of three journeys to Jerusalem (Luke 9:51 — 13:21; John 7:10 — 10:42) begins shortly after Jesus made His secret journey to Jerusalem for the Feast of Tabernacles (John 7:2, 10), after which He presumably returned to Galilee. From Galilee He started to make a journey to Jerusalem (Luke 9:51; John 10:22-39) to eventually attend the Feast of Dedication, December 18, A.D. 32.[75] The ministry between Galilee and Jerusalem was in Samaria (Luke 9:52-56) where He sent out the seventy (Luke 10:1-24) probably into the regions of Samaria and Perea. After their return Jesus had an extensive ministry (Luke 10:25 — 13:21), before arriving in Jerusalem for the Feast of Dedication. This marks the end of the first of these final three journeys to Jerusalem.

After the feast Jesus went to Perea (John 10:40-42). In preparing to return to Jerusalem (Luke 13:22) for His second journey, He had an extensive ministry of miracles and parables probably all in Perea (Luke 13:22 — 17:10). He finally went to Jerusalem to raise Lazarus (John 11:1-54, esp. vv. 7, 17-18). This marks the close of the second of the final three journeys to Jerusalem.

The third journey to Jerusalem is the final one. After raising Lazarus, Jesus went to Ephraim (John 11:54) and from there He possibly continued north to the borders of

[73]Parker and Dubberstein, p. 46.
[74]Wieseler, pp. 316-32.
[75]Parker and Dubberstein, p. 46.

Samaria and Galilee (cf. Luke 17:11 where Samaria is mentioned before Galilee). From there Jesus made His final journey to Jerusalem as is given in Luke 17:11 — 19:28 and is paralleled in Matthew 19:1 — 20:34 and Mark 10:1-52. In His final journey His ministry of miracles and parables was probably accomplished primarily in Perea and Judea. Finally Jesus went to Jerusalem for the Passover (John 11:55 — 12:1) and remained until His death in A.D. 33.[76]

As stated above, there will be those who disagree with the arrangement of the above itinerary; but to fit it into less than a three and a half year period seems highly unlikely. Jesus' ministry, then, began in the summer or autumn of A.D. 29 and came to an end at the Passover of A.D. 33.

[76]The evidence for this will be discussed in chapter V.

Chapter IV

The Day of Christ's Crucifixion

Before one can determine the year of Christ's crucifixion, it is necessary to discuss the day Jesus died. In this chapter, then, there will be a discussion of the day of the week and the day of the Jewish month on which Jesus was crucified. The two problems are quite independent, and hence they will be considered separately.

THE DAY OF THE WEEK

There are three views for the day of Christ's death, namely, the Wednesday, Thursday, and Friday crucifixion.

THE WEDNESDAY CRUCIFIXION

Statement of the view. Those who hold the Wednesday crucifixion view believe that Jesus died around sunset on Wednesday, and He arose exactly seventy-two hours later. The most well-known exponent of this view of recent days is Scroggie.[1] He states that there are two main reasons that support the Wednesday crucifixion date.

The primary support for this view is the literal interpretation of Matthew 12:40 where Jesus states: "For as Jonah was three days and three nights in the belly of the whale; so shall the Son of man be three days and three nights in the heart of the earth." The proponents of this view feel that although it is recognized that the Jews reckoned any part of a day as a whole day, when nights are mentioned as well as days, then it ceases to be an idiom. Therefore, one must accept it literally as three whole days. There are not three

---

[1]W. Graham Scroggie, *A Guide to the Gospels* (London, 1948), pp. 569-77.

whole days between Friday evening and Sunday morning.

The second support for a Wednesday crucifixion is that in the Friday view there are too many events (Scroggie lists twenty)[2] between Christ's death at 3 p.m. and His burial at 6 p.m. Scroggie proposes that Jesus was buried on Wednesday evening, the body remained in the tomb during Thursday, Nisan 15, the Passover Sabbath, and then on Friday, the day between the Sabbaths, the body was embalmed.[3]

In addition to these two main arguments, there is also the argument from typology whereby the lamb was chosen on Nisan 10. In the triumphal entry, Christ, the Lamb of God, appeared in Jerusalem on Saturday, Nisan 10.[4]

Thus, with the literal interpretation of Matthew 12:40, a proper amount of time for the many events between the death and embalmment of Christ, and with the corroborative typology, it is felt that the crucifixion of Christ occurring on Wednesday best satisfies the evidence.

Critique of the view. This view has not been widely accepted. It is not as strong as it might appear. First, it is based primarily on one verse of Scripture, namely, Matthew 12:40. Admittedly, this is the most difficult verse for those who hold to a Friday crucifixion. However, if one looks at other New Testament passages referring to Christ's resurrection, it will be immediately obvious that Jesus rose on the third day and not on the fourth (cf. Matt. 16:21; 17:23; 20:19; 27:64; Luke 9:22; 18:33; 24:7, 21, 46; John 2:19-22; Acts 10:40; 1 Cor. 15:4). Also, it is a well-known fact that the Jews reckoned any part of a day as a *whole* day.

Thus, the three days and three nights in Matthew 12:40 is an idiomatic expression of the same time period (viz., the third day) mentioned in the above cited New Testament passages rather than a literal seventy-two hour period. There will be a more detailed examination of evidence of Jewish reckoning when discussing the Friday view. Suffice it to say here, Matthew 12:40 is not as great an obstacle as the propo-

---

[2]*Ibid.*, pp. 572-73.
[3]*Ibid.*, p. 576.
[4]*Ibid.*, pp. 573-74.

nents of the Wednesday view would have one to believe.

Second, if one takes Matthew 12:40 as referring to a seventy-two hour period, Christ must have risen no later than 6 p.m. on Saturday evening. Otherwise, He would have risen on the fourth day. But Christians celebrate it on the first day of the week (Acts 20:7; 1 Cor. 16:2) and not on the Sabbath.

Third, it is true that many events occurred between Christ's death and burial; but the list is not so great when one examines it, for several things could have been done simultaneously by various people. Also, some things could have been done before He actually died.

Fourth, the corroboration of typology is very weak indeed. This means that Jesus' triumphal entry was on Saturday, the Sabbath. This is unlikely for two reasons: (1) Since Jesus was riding on an animal, He would have been breaking the Mosaic Law which states that even animals were not to work on the Sabbath (Deut. 5:14). (2) Since the people were cutting down branches from the trees (Matt. 21:8; Mark 11:8), they would have also violated the Law (cf. Deut. 5:14; Num. 15:32-36).[5] Certainly if Jesus had violated the Sabbath and caused others to do so, it seems that His enemies would have mentioned something of this during the Passion Week.

Therefore, it is concluded that when one examines all the passages referring to Christ's resurrection, it is evident that Jesus was raised on the third day and not necessarily after seventy-two hours; that Christ's resurrection was on Sunday and not Saturday; that the many events listed by Scroggie could have been accomplished within a short time; and that it is unlikely for Christ's triumphal entry to have occurred on the Sabbath. Hence, the Wednesday view of crucifixion is not a satisfactory solution. In fact, if one did not have Matthew 12:40, it is unlikely that the Wednesday theory would have been suggested.

[5]Cf. Leslie P. Madison, "Problems of Chronology in the Life of Christ" (unpublished Th.D. dissertation, Dallas Theological Seminary, 1963), p. 213.

THE THURSDAY CRUCIFIXION

Statement of the view. As with the previous view, those who hold to a Thursday crucifixion date base their opinion on Matthew 12:40. They think the Friday view has three days but only two nights. The most well-known advocate is Westcott[6] but also it is elaborated in detail by Aldrich[7] and most recently by Rusk.[8] The adherents of the Thursday view would outline the calendar of events as follows: (1) The triumphal entry on Sunday, Nisan 10, would fulfill the Old Testament typology of a Passover lamb selected, namely, Christ Himself. (2) Monday, Tuesday, and Wednesday Jesus appeared in Jerusalem several times and had the Last Supper on Wednesday evening. This, then, eliminates the silent Wednesday of the traditional Friday view. (3) Thursday, Nisan 14, Christ the Passover Lamb was slain. (4) The next day, Nisan 15, was the first day of Unleavened Bread, and this was a day of holy convocation on which no one was to work (Lev. 23:7). Hence, it is concluded that this day of rest is a Sabbath. Thus, when Nisan 15 fell on any other day than the weekly Sabbath, it was called the Sabbath of the Passover. It is felt that John 19:31, which reads: "The day of that Sabbath was a high day" was not the weekly Sabbath but the Passover Sabbath. In the year our Lord was crucified, the Passover Sabbath (Nisan 15) fell on Friday, and then the weekly Sabbath fell on the next day. Also, the advocates point out that the Passover Sabbath on Friday followed immediately by the regular weekly Sabbath is supported by Matthew 28:1. One will notice in the Greek text the plural form of the word "Sabbath" is used, and thus it should be translated "at the end of the Sabbaths."[9] (5) Christ was resurrected early Sunday morning, and thus He was in the

[6]Brooke Foss Westcott, *An Introduction to the Study of the Gospels* (6th ed.; Cambridge and London, 1881), pp. 343-49, esp. pp. 348-49.
[7]J. K. Aldrich, "The Crucifixion on Thursday — Not Friday," *Bibliotheca Sacra*, XXVII (July, 1870), 401-29.
[8]Roger Rusk, "The Day He Died," *Christianity Today*, March 29, 1974, pp. 4-6.
[9]Aldrich, *Bibliotheca Sacra*, XXVII, 424-25; Rusk, p. 5; cf. Westcott, p. 349.

grave three full nights and two full days and a portion of the third day.

Critique of the view. Although the Thursday crucifixion seems to solve the problem of Matthew 12:40, it also has not been widely accepted because there are some real difficulties with the theory. First, it is doubted that anyone would hold to either a Wednesday or Thursday crucifixion date if it were not for Matthew 12:40. When one compares with other Scriptures, the statement in Matthew 12:40 is to be taken as referring to the same time period as the repeated expression in the New Testament "on the third day." This will be discussed in more detail in connection with the Friday crucifixion.

Second, with the Thursday crucifixion date, Christ's triumphal entry on Sunday fulfills the Old Testament typology of being the Passover lamb selected for the Passover. However, there is nothing to prevent the triumphal entry to have occurred on Monday. This would mean not only that Christ was presented as the lamb for Passover on Nisan 10, but also it would eliminate the silent Wednesday which has been criticized against the Friday view by those who hold the Thursday view.

Third, the argument that since Nisan 15 is a holy convocation on which no one works and thus conclude that it was a Sabbath is a *non sequitur.* There is no evidence for this anywhere. This is a creation of those who hold this theory only to fit their theory. Furthermore, to support their theory that John 19:31 ("the day of the Sabbath was great") points to a Passover Sabbath rather than a weekly Sabbath is unlikely. The Friday crucifixion better explains this by seeing that Nisan 15 fell on the weekly Sabbath, and hence in the year of Christ's crucifixion, that weekly Sabbath was indeed great. Further, to think there is support for the Thursday crucifixion in the plural form of the Sabbath in Matthew 28:1 (lit. "at the end of the Sabbaths"), which would indicate that the Passover Sabbath (Friday) and the weekly Sabbath (Saturday) were back to back is untenable. The term Sabbath is frequently (one-third of all of its New Testament occurrences) in the plural form in the New Testament when only one day is in view. For example, in Matthew 12:1-12 both the singular and the plural forms are used (cf. esp. v. 5).[10] There is then no real case for a Passover Sabbath which occurred the day before the regular weekly Sabbath.

Fourth, the Thursday view is forced to make the expression "the day of preparation" ($\pi\alpha\rho\alpha\sigma\kappa\epsilon\nu\dot{\eta}$) refer to the preparations for the Passover rather than its normal usage referring to Friday, the day of preparation for the Sabbath. Those who hold to the Thursday view feel that John 19:14 supports their thesis. It states: "The day of preparation for the Passover" and would indicate the day before the Passover rather than Friday specifically. Hence, according to their view, "the day of preparation" was Thursday and not Friday. But this is unacceptable on three grounds: (1) It necessitates the unnatural meaning of $\pi\alpha\rho\alpha\sigma\kappa\epsilon\nu\dot{\eta}$. Both the Scriptures (Matt. 27:62; Mark 15:42; Luke 23:54; John 19:14, 31, 42) and Josephus[11] indicate the day of preparation is the day before the weekly Sabbaths, namely, Friday. Even Westcott, who holds to a Thursday crucifixion, concedes that the normal use of the phrase refers to Friday.[12] (2) Mark 15:42 exclusively points to "the day of preparation" as being Friday when it states: "and when the evening had come, because it was the day of preparation, that is, *the day before the Sabbath.*" In reading Mark, one sees that he is speaking of the regular weekly Sabbath, and hence the $\pi\alpha\rho\alpha\sigma\kappa\epsilon\nu\dot{\eta}$ refers to Friday. (3) The statement "the day of preparation for the Passover" in John 19:14 seems to have reference to the Friday in the Passover week rather than the day before the Passover. The reason for this is that there is no evidence that the day of preparation for the Passover is the day before the Passover; while there is evidence for $\pi\alpha\rho\alpha\sigma\kappa\epsilon\nu\dot{\eta}$ as being Friday.[13] This is also substantiated in

[10]The weakness of the plural form of the Sabbath is conceded by Aldrich, *Bibliotheca Sacra,* XXVII, 425.
[11]Jos. *Ant.* xvi. 6. 2 § 163.
[12]Westcott, p. 343.
[13]Leon Morris, *The Gospel according to John* (Grand Rapids, 1971), pp. 776-77, 800; A. J. B. Higgins, "The Origins of the Eucharist," *New Testa-*

the immediate context where it specifically states that the bodies should be taken off the cross on the day of preparation so that they would not remain on the cross on the Sabbath, and they put Jesus in the tomb on the "Jewish day of preparation" (John 19:31,42). Certainly in these two verses, παρασκευή is Friday, and the Sabbath refers to the weekly Sabbath.

Therefore, in conclusion the Thursday view has too many problems to make it a real valid solution. Because of not recognizing that the expression three days and three nights in Matthew 12:40 is idiomatic of a three-day period, the Thursday view must propose theories that have far more problems than the one it attempts to solve.

THE FRIDAY CRUCIFIXION

Statement of the view. Jesus predicted that He would die and be raised on the third day (Matt. 16:21; Mark 8:31; Luke 9:22). When one reads these events in the Gospels, one clearly receives the impression that Jesus rose on the third day. Jesus' body was laid in the tomb on the evening of the day of preparation (Friday), the day before the Sabbath (Matt. 27:62; 28:1; Mark 15:42; Luke 23:54, 56; John 19:31, 42). The women returned home and rested on the Sabbath (Saturday, Luke 23:56). Early on the first day of the week (Sunday), they went to the tomb (Matt. 28:1; Mark 16:1-2; Luke 24:1; John 20:1) which was empty. Furthermore, on the same day He arose from the grave, Jesus walked with two disciples on the road to Emmaus (Luke 24:13), and they told Him that their Master was crucified and "now it is the third day since this occurred" (Luke 24:21). This, then, points to His crucifixion as having occurred on Friday. With all this evidence, the only plausible conclusion is that Jesus was crucified on Friday and rose on Sunday.

---

ment Studies, I (April, 1955), 206-8; Charles C. Torrey, "The Date of the Crucifixion according to the Fourth Gospel," *Journal of Biblical Literature*, L (December, 1931), 233-37; Charles C. Torrey, "In the Fourth Gospel the Last Supper was the Paschal Meal," *The Jewish Quarterly Review*, XLII (January, 1952), 239-40.

This view also fits well with Old Testament typology. On Monday, Nisan 10, Jesus presented Himself as the Paschal lamb at the triumphal entry. On Nisan 14 He was sacrificed as the Paschal lamb (1 Cor. 5:7), and on Nisan 16 His resurrection was a type of the offering of First Fruits (1 Cor. 15:23).

In conclusion then, with the most natural reading of the New Testament, one would conclude that Jesus was crucified on Friday and was resurrected on Sunday. This is also the common consensus of the Church Fathers and scholars throughout church history, and it is the view generally accepted today.

Critique of the view. The one problem that is proposed against the Friday view is Matthew 12:40, that He would be in the heart of the earth for three days and three nights. Admittedly, this is the most difficult verse for those who hold the Friday view, but it is not as formidable as it first appears. One must examine all the evidence at hand. First to be discussed is the New Testament evidence. The most frequent reference to Jesus' resurrection is that it occurred on the third day (not the fourth day) (Matt. 16:21; 17:23; 20:19; 27:64; Luke 9:22; 18:33; 24:7, 21, 46; Acts 10:40; 1 Cor. 15:4). In John 2:19-22, where Jesus spoke of His resurrection, He stated that He would be raised up in three days and not on the fourth day. There are four passages (Matt. 27:63; Mark 8:31; 9:31; 10:34) which speak of Christ's resurrection as occurring "after three days," but this is speaking of the same time period as on "the third day" for the following two reasons: (1) The three Markan passages are paralleled by one or two of the other Synoptic Gospels, and in each case the other Synoptic does not use "after three days" as Mark does but "on the third day" (Mark 8:31 = Matt. 16:21/Luke 9:22; Mark 9:31 = Matt. 17:23; Mark 10:34 = Matt. 20:19/Luke 18:33). Thus, the two phrases mean a period extending to the third day. (2) In Matthew 27:63 where the Pharisees before Pilate state that Jesus had predicted that "after three days I will rise again," the Pharisees then asked Pilate if they could have a guard of soldiers to secure the sepulcher until the third day. The phrase "after three days" must have been equivalent to "the third day," or otherwise the Pharisees would have asked for a guard of soldiers until the fourth day.[14]

Having looked at the New Testament evidence,[15] one must ask whether or not this was standard Jewish thinking. If one looks in both the Old Testament and Rabbinic literature, one sees that it would agree with the New Testament evidence. Therefore, the next piece of evidence to be examined is the Old Testament. There are several Old Testament references which show that a part of a day is equivalent to the whole day. In Genesis 42:17 Joseph incarcerated his brothers for three days, and then in verse 18 he spoke to them on the third day, and (from the context) released them on that day. In 1 Kings 20:29 Israel and Syria camped opposite each other for seven days, and on the seventh day they began to battle each other. In 2 Chronicles 10:5 Rehoboam stated that the people of Israel were to return to him in/after (cf. LXX) three days, and in verse 12 Jeroboam and the people came to Rehoboam on the third day. In Esther 4:16 Esther asks the Jews, "Do not eat or drink for three days, night or day," and then she would go in to the king, and in 5:1 Esther went in to the king on the third day. Finally, in 1 Samuel 30:12 an abandoned Egyptian servant had not eaten bread or drunk water for three days and three nights, and in verse 13 he states that his master left him behind three days ago. Thus, the Old Testament gives the picture that the expressions "three days," "the third day," and "three days and three nights" are used to signify the same period of time.

Having seen that the Old Testament evidence agrees with the New, the final piece of evidence to be examined is the Rabbinic literature. It is interesting to note that the same

[14]Possibly some could argue the fourth day after Jesus' death is meant since the request was made on the day after His death. But it seems more likely that the Pharisees were reckoning from the date of Christ's death. It is interesting to note that in all other instances Matthew uses the phrase "on the third day" and never "after three days." Thus it seems that the Pharisees were reckoning from Jesus' death.
[15]For usage in Greek literature outside the New Testament, see Frederick Field, *Notes on Select Passages of the Greek Testament* (Oxford, 1881), pp. 8-9.

concept is borne out in Rabbinic literature. There are several passages found in Jewish literature which combine Jonah 1:17 ("Jonah was in the belly of the fish three days and three nights") with the Old Testament passages listed in the above paragraph.[16] Furthermore, Rabbi Eleazar ben Azariah (lived *ca.* A.D. 100), who was the tenth in the descent from Ezra, stated: "A day and night are an Onah ['a portion of time'] and the portion of an Onah is as the whole of it."[17]

In conclusion, when one examines all the evidence, it seems that the New Testament, the Old Testament, and Rabbinic literature all agree that a part of a day is counted as a whole day-and-night. Thus, the expressions: "the three days and three nights," "after three days," and "on the third day" are all one and the same time span. These all support the fact that Christ was crucified on Friday and was resurrected on Sunday.

CONCLUSION

Having examined the three different views, it was concluded that the Friday date for the crucifixion is the most acceptable. Both the Wednesday and Thursday views are basically built on one verse, namely, Matthew 12:40. These views are untenable because, first, the preponderance of Scripture would indicate Jesus' crucifixion as having occurred on Friday, and, second, when one realizes that the Jews reckoned a part of a day as a whole day, these options no longer stand. Furthermore, the Friday crucifixion view has had the overwhelming support of scholars throughout the history of the church.

THE DAY OF THE MONTH

Having concluded that Friday was the day of Christ's crucifixion, it is now the place to discuss the day(s) of the month on which Christ ate the last Passover and was crucified.

[16]Midrash Rabbah: Genesis lvi. 1 (on Gen. 22:4); Genesis xci. 7 (on Gen. 42:17-18); Esther ix. 2 (on Esther 5:1); Midrash on the Psalms: Ps. 22:5.
[17]Jerusalem Talmud: Shabbath ix. 3; cf. also Babylonian Talmud: Pesahim 4*a*.

THE PROBLEM OF THE DATE

All the Gospels state that Jesus ate the Last Supper the day before His crucifixion (Matt. 26:20; Mark 14:17; Luke 22:14; John 13:2; cf. also 1 Cor. 11:23). However, according to Mark 14:12 the Last Supper was "on the first day of Unleavened Bread, when they sacrificed the Passover lamb," when the disciples went and made preparation for Jesus "to eat the Passover." The other two Synoptics (Matt. 26:17; Luke 22:7-8) state essentially the same thing. Therefore, the Synoptics portray that the Last Supper was the Passover meal celebrated on Thursday evening and that Jesus was crucified the following day, namely, Friday, Nisan 15.

On the other hand, John states that the Jews who took Jesus to the Praetorium did not enter it "in order that they might not be defiled but might eat the Passover" (John 18:28). This means that Jesus was tried and crucified before the time the Jews had the Passover. This is substantiated in John 19:14 where it states that Jesus' trial and crucifixion were on the "day of preparation for the Passover" and not after the eating of the Passover. Therefore, it appears that Jesus' Last Supper (which occurred on Thursday night) was not a Passover and that Jesus was tried and crucified on Friday, Nisan 14, just before the eating of the Passover. This is substantiated by Paul when he mentions that Christ, our Paschal Lamb, has been sacrificed (1 Cor. 5:7), as well as the Gospel of Peter that says that Jesus was delivered to the people "on the day before the Unleavened Bread, their feast"[18] and by the Babylonian Talmud, which probably refers to Christ when it says: "On the eve of the Passover, Yeshu (ms. M: the Nazarean) was hanged."[19]

Therefore, the Synoptics see Jesus celebrating the Last Supper as a Passover meal on Thursday, Nisan 14, with the trial and crucifixion on Friday, Nisan 15, whereas in John the Last Supper was not a Passover meal, celebrated on Thurs-

[18]Gospel of Peter 6.
[19]Babylonian Talmud: Sanhedrin 43*a*.

day, Nisan 13, with the trial and crucifixion on Friday, Nisan 14. Christ, then, was crucified at the same time as the Paschal lambs were slain.

THE PROBLEM OF THE LAST SUPPER

Introduction. The instructions for the Passover were given at the time that the Israelites were leaving Egypt (Exod. 12; cf. also Lev. 23:4-8; Num. 9:3-14; Deut. 16:1-8). On the tenth day of the first month (Nisan = March/April), a lamb was selected for each household (Exod. 12:3). On Nisan 14 the lamb was slain "between the two evenings" (Exod. 12:6; Lev. 23:5; Num. 9:3, 5) which according to Josephus was between the ninth and eleventh hours,[20] that is, from 3 to 5 p.m. Then, in "that night" the Passover meal was eaten (Exod. 12:8).

The Last Supper was a Passover. In the attempt to solve the dilemma, one must first settle whether or not the Last Supper was a Passover. Many believe that it was the Passover meal. In summary form, the scholars[21] list the following arguments for a Passover meal: (1) the Synoptics explicitly state that the Last Supper was a Passover (Matt. 26:2, 17, 18, 19; Mark 14:1, 12, 14, 16; Luke 22:1, 7, 8, 13, 15). (2) It took place, as required by the Law (Deut. 16:7), within the gates of Jerusalem even though it was so crowded at the time. (3) The Upper Room was made available without difficulty in keeping with the Passover custom. (4) The Last Supper was eaten at night (Matt. 26:20; Mark 14:17; John 13:30; 1 Cor. 11:23) which was an unusual time for a meal. (5) Jesus limited Himself to the twelve rather than eating with the large circle of followers (which corresponds to the Passover custom). (6) A reclining posture at the table was for

[20]Jos. *BJ* vi. 9. 3 § 423.
[21]For further details, see Joachim Jeremias, *The Eucharistic Words of Jesus*, trans. by Norman Perrin (London, 1966), pp. 41-56; A. J. B. Higgins, *The Lord's Supper in the New Testament* (London, 1952), pp. 20-23; Gustaf Dalman, *Jesus-Jeshua*, trans. by Paul P. Levertoff (London, 1929), pp. 106-32; Morris, pp. 774-75; E. Robinson, "The Alleged Discrepancy between John and the Other Evangelists respecting Our Lord's Last Passover," *Bibliotheca Sacra*, II (August, 1845), 406-36.

special occasions only. (7) The meal was eaten in Levitical purity (John 13:10). (8) Jesus broke the bread during the meal (Matt. 26:26; Mark 14:22) rather than as customarily done at the beginning of the meal. (9) Red wine was drunk which was only for special occasions. (10) Some of the disciples thought that Judas left (John 13:29) to purchase items for the feast which would not have been necessary if the Last Supper was a day before the Passover since he would have had the whole next day (Nisan 14) available for this purpose. (11) Some of the disciples thought that Judas left to give to the poor (John 13:29) which was customary on Passover night. (12) The Last Supper ends with the singing of a hymn which would have been the second half of the Passover *hallel*. (13) Jesus did not return to Bethany which was outside of Jerusalem's limit but went to spend the night on the Mount of Olives which was within the enlarged city limits for the purpose of the Passover feast. (14) The interpretation of specific elements of the meal was a part of the Passover ritual.

These arguments are very forceful and seem to make good sense.

The Last Supper was not a Passover. There are, however, some scholars who think the Last Supper was not a Passover. They would raise the following objections:[22] (1) John's order of events would seem to indicate that the Lord's Supper was a day before the Passover. John 13:1 states: "Now before the Feast of Passover, when Jesus knew that his hour was come that he should depart out of this world." However, this does not seem to refer to the Last Supper as occurring before the Passover, but rather that Jesus "knew" before the Passover that His death was immi-

---

[22]For a fuller treatment, see Jeremias, pp. 62-84; A. J. B. Higgins, *The Lord's Supper*, pp. 16-20; George Ogg, "The Chronology of the Last Supper," *Historicity and Chronology in the New Testament* (London, 1965), pp. 76-77; cf. also William Frederick, "Did Jesus Eat the Passover?" *Bibliotheca Sacra*, LXVIII (July, 1911), 503-9. Stauffer thinks that since Jesus was considered a preacher of apostasy, He would not have been allowed by the temple officials to have a paschal lamb slain. Ethelbert Stauffer, *Jesus and His Story*, trans. by Dorothea M. Barton (London, 1960), pp. 94-95.

nent.[23] In the same chapter, John says, "For some of them thought, because Judas had the bag, that Jesus had said unto him, 'Buy those things we need for the feast' " (John 13:29). But if this were Nisan 13, there would be no need to buy the festival items that night because the whole of the next day (Nisan 14) would be available for that purpose. This verse makes sense only on the evening of Nisan 14 for one would not be able to buy on Nisan 15, a high feast day.[24] Later, John remarks: "Then they led Jesus from the house of Caiaphas to the Praetorium; and it was early, and they themselves did not enter the Praetorium in order that they might not be defiled but might eat the Passover" (John 18:28). Therefore, Jesus had already the night before participated in the Last Supper. This is substantiated by John 19:14 where it states, "Now it was the day of preparation of the Passover." But as discussed in the first part of this chapter, this phrase means nothing more than "Friday of the Passover week." Finally, John 19:36 speaks of the fulfillment of the Old Testament (Exod. 12:46; Num. 9:12) when no bones of Jesus, the Passover Lamb, were broken. Jesus, then, was slain when the other Paschal lambs were slain, and hence, the Last Supper was before Passover. Both John 18:28 and 19:36 will be discussed below.

This first argument is the basic one. The others following that substantiate it are: (2) The bread is spoken of as $\check{\alpha}\rho\tau\sigma\varsigma$ not as $\check{\alpha}\zeta\nu\mu\alpha$ (unleavened bread). However, unleavened bread was commonly called "bread." (3) No mention is made of the Paschal lamb and the bitter herbs. But the Passover was so familiar there was no need to mention all the elements. Furthermore, the Passover lamb may have been referred to in Luke 22:15.[25] (4) Only a single cup is denoted instead of individual Passover cups. In Jesus' day, however, a common cup was used in celebrating the Passover. (5) The Synoptics specifically state that Jesus was not to be arrested

[23]Cf. Torrey, *The Jewish Quarterly Review*, XLII, 245-48.
[24]Robinson, *Bibliotheca Sacra*, VII, 426-27; Jeremias, p. 53.
[25]Cf. C. K. Barrett, "Luke XXII. 15: To Eat the Passover," *The Journal of Theological Studies*, IX (October, 1958), 305-7.

during the feast (Matt. 26:5; Mark 14:2). But it makes more sense to say "the Jews sought Jesus among the festal crowd" ($\mu\dot{\eta}$ $\dot{\epsilon}\nu$ $\tau\tilde{\eta}$ $\dot{\epsilon}o\rho\tau\tilde{\eta}$)[26] because by this time a great number of pilgrims had already arrived for purification (John 11:55), and hence it would have already been "during the feast." (6) The Passover was a traditional family meal where the father presided whereas at the Last Supper no women were present, and it is Jesus, not a father, who presides. Granted, there were normally members of the family present, but this being of special significance for Jesus to be with His disciples at that hour may have eliminated normal family relationships. From the text, one cannot argue for or against the presence of women. Neither is there the necessity of a mixed group. (7) A number of events that happened the day after the Lord's Supper were forbidden on a feast day, such as, leaving Jerusalem to go to Gethsemane, carrying of arms, the session of the Sanhedrin and the condemnation of Christ on the very night of the Passover, the coming of Simon from the fields which indicates he had been working, the purchase of linen by Joseph of Arimathea on the evening of the feast, and the burial of the body on the feast day. All of these have been adequately answered by Dalman and Billerbeck.[27] Briefly, Jerusalem could not be left during Passover, but its borders were enlarged during the Passover, which included Gethsemane. The Jews were allowed to carry arms on Sabbaths (and on feast days).[28] The Law (Deut. 17:12) prescribed the death penalty for anyone who opposes priests and judges. The Jewish Law states that a rebellious teacher of the Law could be executed on a feast day.[29] We need not assume that Simon worked, especially since it was early in the morning (Mark 15:25). More likely, it means he came in from the country.[30] The purchases of Joseph of Arimathea

[26]For a discussion of this, see Jeremias, pp. 71-73.
[27]Dalman, pp. 93-106; Hermann L. Strack and Paul Billerbeck, *Kommentar zum Neuen Testament* (München, 1924), II, 815-34.
[28]Mishnah: Shabbath vi. 4.
[29]Mishnah: Sanhedrin xi. 4.
[30]Dalman, pp. 100-101; Strack-Billerbeck, II, 828-29.

were proper for necessities could be obtained on the Sabbath (and on a feast day).[31] And finally, the burial of a body was to be done on the same day as the death (Deut. 21:23). (8) There is a Jewish tradition that Jesus was executed on the eve of the Passover.[32] This may be a polemic to indicate that Jesus, the false teacher, did not partake of the Passover and was properly executed according to their laws.

Those who conclude that the Last Supper was not the Passover have difficulty in trying to identify the meal. There have been two suggestions. First, there is the theory which was made prominent by Box[33] which identifies it with the ceremony known as *kiddush* or sanctification.[34] It was a ceremony which pronounced blessings at the commencement of each Sabbath and feast day. This view is untenable for the sanctification of Passover did not occur twenty-four hours before its commencement. Rather at the opening of the Passover meal *kiddush* was said over the first cup.[35] Second, Lietzmann suggested that the Last Supper was a *haburah* meal which was a meal partaken by a small company of like-minded friends.[36] But there is no evidence that Jesus and His followers formed such a group. Furthermore, the circle of friends who had these *haburah* meals "were exclusively *duty* meals such as those connected with betrothals, weddings, circumcisions, funerals in which participation as a paying guest was considered meritorious."[37] Certainly, this is not the picture of the Last Supper.

In conclusion, one sees that any theory which makes the Last Supper not the Passover meal, does not give a satisfactory identification of the meal. Again, considering all of the evidence, it seems to be best to accept the Last Supper as having been a Passover meal.

[31]Mishnah: Shabbath xxiii. 4.
[32]Babylonian Talmud: Sanhedrin 43*a*.
[33]G. H. Box, "The Jewish Antecedents of the Eucharist," *The Journal of Theological Studies,* III (April, 1902), 357-69.
[34]Cf. Jeremias, pp. 26-29.
[35]Mishnah: Pesahim x. 2.
[36]Hans Lietzmann, *Mass and Lord's Supper,* trans. by Dorothea H. G. Reeve (London, 1953-54), pp. 170-71.
[37]Jeremias, p. 30.

THE PROBLEM OF HARMONIZATION

There are several options that have been offered. First, some scholars feel that the Synoptics and John cannot be harmonized with the result that some prefer the Synoptics over John while others prefer John over the Synoptics. Some feel that John is correct and the Synoptics are to be interpreted accordingly. This view holds that the Last Supper was not the Passover. The untenableness of this view has already been discussed. Some feel that the Synoptics are right and John needs to be interpreted accordingly. This view accepts the Last Supper as having been a Passover meal. This is plausible but still does not adequately explain two passages of Scripture, namely: (1) John 18:28 which states that the Jews did not enter the Praetorium "in order that they might not be defiled, but might eat the Passover." If Jesus' Last Supper was the Passover, how on the next day could the Jews say they had not eaten the Passover?[38] Geldenhuys suggests (as did Zahn earlier) that this does not have reference to the meal but to keep the Feast of Unleavened Bread or one of the sacrificial meals in that week.[39] But Morris has given a death blow to this theory when he states that one may concede that "the Passover" can refer to the Passover plus the Feast of Unleavened Bread, but certainly it cannot refer to the Feast of Unleavened Bread without the Passover, which is what is required if one accepts this theory.[40] (2) John 19:36 speaks of the Old Testament fulfillment when no bones of Jesus, the Passover Lamb, were broken.

The first of these two passages is far more significant than the second. It is the Achilles' heel of this view when trying to interpret John in accordance with the Synoptics. Therefore, a fourth solution is needed, namely that both the Synoptics and John are correct. Again, various attempts have been made here. Some think that Jesus anticipated that

[38]Note Jeremias' struggle with the passage (pp. 79-82).
[39]Norval Geldenhuys, *Commentary on the Gospel of Luke* (London, 1950), pp. 649-70, esp. pp. 661-63.
[40]Morris, pp. 778-79.

He was going to be killed at the Passover season; so with His disciples He had His own private Passover a day early.[41] But this is impossible since the Passover lamb had to be slaughtered within the temple precincts. None of the officials would have done this for that would be against the regulations.[42] Hence, Christ and the disciples would not have had a Passover lamb for the Passover meal. This is inconceivable. Certainly, the Gospels picture that Christ and the disciples had a Passover lamb, and it had already been slaughtered (Mark 14:12-16; Luke 22:7-13; cf. also Matt. 26:17-19). Second to be considered is a rather recent theory proposed by Jaubert[43] and followed by Ruckstuhl.[44] Jaubert thinks that Jesus' Last Supper was a Passover meal, but following the Qumran calendar, He celebrated it on the Tuesday of Passion Week, and yet following the official calendar, Christ was crucified on Friday when the Passover lambs were slain. This accepts the best of both worlds. However, there is no indication that Jesus was really associated with or ministered to the Qumran community and certainly no indication in the Gospels to support the conclusion that Jesus ever followed a Qumran calendar.[45]

Third, some think that the Jews in Jesus' day celebrated the Passover on two consecutive days. Chwolson assumes that the Paschal lambs were slain "between the two evenings" (i.e., 3 to 5 p.m.) on Nisan 14 as commanded in the Old Testament (Exod. 12:6; Lev. 23:5; Num. 9:3, 5). Since in the

[41]Cf. Reginald H. Fuller, *The Mission and Achievement of Jesus* (London, 1954), pp. 70-71; Vincent Taylor, *The Gospel according to St. Mark* (2nd ed.; London, 1966), pp. 664-67.
[42]Mishnah: Zebahim i. 3.
[43]Annie Jaubert, *The Date of the Last Supper*, trans. by Isaac Rafferty (New York, 1965).
[44]Eugen Ruckstuhl, *Chronology of the Last Days of Jesus*, trans. by Victor J. Drapela (New York, 1965).
[45]For a critique of her view, see Josef Blinzler, "Qumran-Kalendar und Passionchronologie," *Zeitschrift für die neutestamentliche Wissenschaft*, XLIX (1958), 238-51; George Ogg, "Review of Mlle Jaubert, *La date de la Cène*," *Novum Testamentum*, III (January, 1959), 149-60; Norman Walker, "Pauses in the Passion Story and their Significance for Chronology," *Novum Testamentum*, VI (January, 1963), 16-19; Jeremias, pp. 24-25.

year in which Jesus died Nisan 14 was a Friday, and since not all the Paschal lambs could be slain before the Sabbath (Nisan 15) began, they were slain on Thursday evening (Nisan 13). Because Exodus 12:10 states that the Passover was to be eaten the night it was slain, the Pharisees celebrated the Passover immediately (Nisan 13/14) while the Sadducees waited until the usual time (i.e., Nisan 14/15). Hence, Jesus and His disciples celebrated the Passover with the Pharisees on Thursday night (Nisan 13/14) while the Jews mentioned in John 18:28 were of the Sadducees who would not have eaten the Passover until Friday night (Nisan 14/15).[46] The problems of the theory are as follows: (1) Would the Sadducees not have obeyed Exodus 12:10? (2) Would Jesus have celebrated the Passover on Nisan 13/14 when the Law specified Nisan 14/15? (3) Jesus would not have been able to eat it with unleavened bread since that feast did not begin until the evening of Nisan 14/15 which would have changed the whole character of the Passover ritual. (4) According to Jeremias, there is evidence that when Nisan 15 was a Sabbath, the Jews could slaughter the victims earlier in the afternoon.[47]

Billerbeck has modified Chwolson's theory.[48] He thinks that there was a difference of one day between the Boethusian/Sadducean party and the Pharisees. Billerbeck gives evidence of their difference of interpretation in reckoning the fifty days forward to Pentecost from the Sunday in Passover Week or Nisan 16.[49] Leviticus 23:15 states: "You shall account unto you from the morrow after the Sabbath." The Pharisees would interpret the term "Sabbath" to mean

[46]D. Chwolson, *Das letzte Passamahl Christi und der Tag seines Todes* (2nd ed.; Leipzig, 1908), pp. 20-44. Cf. also Joséph Klausner, *Jesus of Nazareth*, trans. by Herbert Danby (London, 1925), pp. 326-28; M.-J. Lagrange, *The Gospel of Jesus Christ*, trans. by Members of the English Dominican Province (London, 1938), II, 193-96.
[47]Jeremias, p. 23.
[48]Strack-Billerbeck, II, 812-53; cf. also W. M. Christie, "Did Christ Eat the Passover with His Disciples? or, The Synoptics *versus* John's Gospel," *The Expository Times*, XLIII (August, 1932), 515-19; J. B. Segal, *The Hebrew Passover* (London, 1963), pp. 241-69.
[49]Strack-Billerbeck, II, 847-50; cf. also J. van Goudoever, *Biblical Calendars* (2nd ed.; Leiden, 1961), pp. 15-29.

"festival" (i.e., Passover) and would count from the day following the Passover regardless of what day it was in the week. On the other hand, the Sadducees interpreted "Sabbath" literally and would count from the Sunday after the Passover.[50] Therefore, in the year Christ died, the Boethusian/Sadducean party was anxious to have Nisan 16 fall on Sunday, and the priestly calendar commission agreed to fix the beginning of Nisan so that the Nisan 14 would be a Friday and Nisan 16 a Sunday, and consequently Pentecost would fall on Sunday. However, the Pharisees reckoned the month to have begun one day ealier. A compromise resulted which meant that the Boethusian/Sadducean party celebrated Passover on Friday evening, Nisan 14, according to the calendar commission, while the Pharisees, and with them Jesus and His disciples, celebrated on Thursday evening (Nisan 14 according to the Pharisaic reckoning). Thus, in the year Christ died, there were two consecutive days for Passover.[51] This theory has more merit than Chwolson's in that both parties celebrated the Passover of Nisan 14/15, and the Feast of Unleavened Bread could be used by both parties. The main problem is that it rests on the conjecture that there was a debate over the commencement of Nisan in the year Christ died.

Pickl suggests that since there were so many pilgrims it would be impossible to slaughter all the lambs and to have enough houses in Jerusalem for the purpose of eating the Passover. So there arose the custom where the Galileans slew their lambs on Nisan 13, and the Feast of Unleavened Bread lasted eight days whereas the Judeans celebrated on Nisan 14.[52] This makes good sense except as Jeremias has pointed out that his basis of the eight-day Feast of Un-

[50]Mishnah: Hagigah ii. 4; Menahoth x. 3.
[51]Strack-Billerbeck, II, 850-53. Shepherd has similar arguments except he argues that John followed the reckoning of the month according to the Palestinian method whereas the Synoptics followed the calendar of the Diaspora Judaism, Massey Shepherd, Jr., "Are both the Synoptics and John Correct about the Date of Jesus' Death?" *Journal of Biblical Literature,* LXXX (March, 1961), 123-32.
[52]Josef Pickl, *The Messias,* trans. by Andrew Green (St. Louis, 1946), pp. 120-22.

leavened Bread is a practice of the diaspora "where the Jews celebrated all festivals one day longer than in Palestine."[53]

Finally, one should consider that there are different ways to reckon a day. This is a puzzling problem that has set many pens into motion. It is beyond the scope of this chapter to go into a lengthy discussion of the reckoning of days. Only a summarization can be given.[54]

First to be considered is the reckoning from sunset to sunset. There is the Feast of Unleavened Bread which runs from evening to evening, of Nisan 14 to the evening of Nisan 21 (Exod. 12:18). This is also true of the Day of Atonement (Lev. 23:32), the weekly Sabbath (Neh. 13:19), and when there is a single day's ceremonial uncleanness, it ends at the evening (Lev. 11; 14:46; 15; 17:15; 22:6; Deut. 23:11). The order in which the evening and morning are listed would indicate that days began with the sunset (cf. Deut. 1:33; 28:66; 1 Sam. 25:16; 1 Kings 8:29; Esther 4:16; Mark 4:27; 5:5; Luke 2:37; etc.).[55]

Second, there is also the reckoning from sunrise to sunrise. Both Zeitlin[56] and de Vaux[57] conclude that the Jews reckoned from morning to morning before the exile and evening to evening after the exile, but the passages listed above would argue against the validity of this. However,

---

[53]Jeremias, p. 24.

[54]For a more detailed study of the problem, see Julian Morgenstern, "Supplementary Studies in the Calendars of Ancient Israel," *Hebrew Union College Annual*, X (1935), 15-28; P. J. Heawood, "The Beginning of the Jewish Day," *The Jewish Quarterly Review*, XXXVI (April, 1945), 393-401; Solomon Zeitlin, "The Beginning of the Jewish Day during the Second Commonwealth," *The Jewish Quarterly Review*, XXXVI (April, 1945), 403-14; Jack Finegan, *Handbook of Biblical Chronology* (Princeton, 1964), pp. 7-15; H. R. Stroes, "Does the Day Begin in the Evening or Morning?" *Vetus Testamentum*, XVI (October, 1966), 460-75; Roger T. Beckwith, "The Day, its Divisions and its Limits, in Biblical Thought," *The Evangelical Quarterly*, XLIII (October-December, 1971), 218-27.

[55]For more detail, see Beckwith, *The Evangelical Quarterly*, XLIII, 221-24.

[56]Zeitlin, *The Jewish Quarterly Review*, XXXVI, 403-14.

[57]Roland de Vaux, *Ancient Israel: Its Life and Institutions*, trans. by John McHugh (London, 1961), pp. 180-83.

there are some indications that they reckoned from sunrise to sunrise. There are references of the day listed before night (Gen. 1:14, 16, 18; 8:22; 31:40; Num. 14:14; 2 Sam. 21:10; 1 Kings 8:59; Neh. 1:6; 4:9; Luke 18:7; Acts 9:24; Rev. 4:8; etc.). Also, when the expressions "the same day" or "the next day" are used, the context clearly indicates that the night belongs to the first day and not the beginning of a new day (cf. Gen. 19:34; 1 Sam. 19:11; Acts 4:3; 20:7-11; 23:32; etc.).[58] The one passage in the New Testament that may more explicitly indicate a sunrise-to-sunrise reckoning is Matthew 28:1 where it states that the women came to the tomb "late on the Sabbath as it began to dawn towards the first day of the week." Thus the new day began with sunrise. However, as Beckwith points out, this could be translated "*after* the Sabbath day, as it began to dawn *on* the first day of the week."[59] Regarding the Passover, one can also see a sunrise-to-sunrise reckoning in Deuteronomy 16:4 where it states nothing which is sacrificed on the evening of the first day shall remain overnight until morning.

In conclusion, one sees that both reckonings were used even by some authors within the same book.

But what about the Passover of Jesus' day? As indicated above, the Passover could be reckoned from sunset to sunset or sunrise to sunrise. Generally, it is thought it was reckoned from sunset to sunset. Yet Josephus, who was a Pharisee living in Jesus' day, in explaining the law of the Passover, states that the Paschal lamb must be eaten during the night with nothing left for the morning.[60] This seems to indicate a sunrise-to-sunrise reckoning. The Mishnah states that the Passover lamb must be eaten by midnight[61] which would seem to indicate that the new day began after sunset, namely, at sunrise.

Since in Jesus' day there were two systems of reckoning the day, it is thought by several that this would be a

[58]For more detail, see Beckwith, *The Evangelical Quarterly*, XLIII, 224-25.
[59]*Ibid.*, XLIII, 226.
[60]Jos. *Ant.* iii. 10. 5 § 248.
[61]Mishnah: Pesahim x. 9; Zebahim v. 8.

solution to the disagreement between the Synoptics and John. It is thought that the Galileans used a different method of reckoning the Passover than the Judeans. The Galileans and Pharisees used the sunrise-to-sunrise reckoning whereas the Judeans and Sadducees used the sunset-to-sunset reckoning.[62] Thus, according to the Synoptics, the Last Supper was a Passover meal. Since the day was to be reckoned from sunrise, the Galileans, and with them Jesus and His disciples, had the Paschal lamb slaughtered in the late afternoon of Thursday, Nisan 14, and later that evening they ate the Passover with the unleavened bread.[63] On the other hand, the Judean Jews who reckoned from sunset to sunset would slay the lamb on Friday afternoon which marked the end of Nisan 14 and would eat the Passover lamb with the unleavened bread that night which had become Nisan 15. Thus, Jesus had eaten the Passover meal when His enemies, who had not as yet had the Passover, arrested Him.

This interpretation eliminates the difficulties presented in John's Gospel. First, this gives good sense to John 18:28 where the Jews did not want to enter the Praetorium so as not to be defiled since later that day they would slay the victims for those who reckoned from sunset-to-sunset. Second, John 19:14 makes sense for it says that Jesus' trial and crucifixion were on the "day of preparation for the Passover" and not after the eating of the Passover. Third, this fits well with John 19:36 where it speaks of the fulfillment of the Old Testament (Exod. 12:46; Num. 9:12) when no bones of Jesus, the Passover Lamb, were broken. After Jesus' trial and crucifixion, He died when the Paschal lambs were slain in the temple precincts.

[62] Julian Morgenstern, "The Calendar of the Book of Jubilees, its Origin and its Character," *Vetus Testamentum*, V (January, 1955), 64-65 n. 2; Finegan, pp. 452-53; G. R. Driver, "Two Problems in the New Testament," *The Journal of Theological Studies*, XVI (October, 1965), 327.
[63] In the New Testament the first day of Unleavened Bread is Nisan 14 and not Nisan 15 (Matt. 26:17; Mark 14:12; Luke 22:7) which according to Beckwith (*The Evangelical Quarterly*, XLIII, 222 n. 4) is a later custom seen in the Mishnah for they prepared for the Feast of Unleavened Bread by removing all the leaven from one's house on Nisan 14 (Mishnah: Pesahim i. 1-5; iii. 6; v. 4). Cf. also Segal, pp. 244-45.

This view not only satisfies the data of the Synoptics and the Gospel of John, it is also substantiated by the Mishnah. It was the custom of the Galileans to do no work on the day of the Passover while the Judeans worked until midday.[64] Since the Galileans' day began at sunrise they would do no work on the entire day of the Passover. On the other hand the Judeans' day began at sunset and they would work the morning but not the afternoon. Their ceasing to work at midday could have been either the Judeans' Nisan 14 which would have given them time for slaying their Paschal lambs that afternoon or more probably the midday of the Judeans' Nisan 13, which meant that they did not work in deference to the Galileans' Nisan 14 (who would have been slaying their Paschal lambs that afternoon). If the latter view is accepted then the order of events would be as following (using the Galilean reckoning): (1) on the morning of Nisan 14 no Galilean would be working; (2) the Judeans would cease working by midday; and (3) the Galileans would slay their Paschal lambs later that afternoon.

In conclusion, then, the proposed interpretation does justice to the data of the Synoptics, the Gospel of John, and the Mishnah. It can be charted as shown on the next page.

This solution means that there were two days of slaughter. This would solve the problem of having to slaughter all of the lambs for all of those participants at the Passover season.

There are two problems with this theory. First is the problem of having two consecutive days of slaughtering Paschal lambs. Would the Sadducees allow this since they were in control of the temple? It is possible they had to. It is known that with the popular support the Pharisees had, the Sadducees would submit to their wishes at times.[65] Finkel states that "the Pharisees determined the dates of the great festivals."[66] Here may be a case in point where neither party compromised and so there were two days of Passover

64Mishnah: Pesahim iv. 5.
65Jos. *Ant.* xviii. 1. 4 § 17; Babylonian Talmud: Yoma 19*b*.
66Asher Finkel, *The Pharisees and the Teacher of Nazareth* (Leiden, 1964), p. 74.

THE RECKONING OF PASSOVER

THURSDAY	Galilean Method Synoptic Reckoning Used by Jesus, His Disciples, and Pharisees	Judean Method John's Reckoning Used by Sadducees	Midnight
	Nisan 14		Sunrise
	3-5 P.M. Passover Lamb Slain		
Last Supper		Nisan 14	Sunset
Jesus Arrested			Midnight
FRIDAY			
6 A.M. Jesus before Pilate	Nisan 15		Sunrise
9 A.M. Crucifixion			
12-3 P.M. Darkness			
3 P.M. Jesus Died		3-5 P.M. Passover Lamb Slain	
Jesus Buried		Nisan 15	Sunset
SATURDAY			Midnight

slaughter. The second problem with the theory is that there is no explicit statement to support the view. Although one cannot be overly dogmatic, it does fit well with the data at hand. It is simple and makes good sense.

CONCLUSION

It was the purpose of this section of the chapter to look at the problem of the day of the Jewish month posed by the Synoptics and John. It was concluded that Jesus ate the Passover. Having accepted this as the correct rendering, then the problem of harmonization was discussed. Different attempts have been made. It is generally accepted that different calendars for reckoning the Passover were used by various groups and regions.[67] This makes it difficult to know which ones were in operation during the time of the last week of Christ's ministry.

Of all the suggestions given, it was felt that Billerbeck's theory has great merit. However, in looking over the data, it was felt that the most tenable solution is to recognize that the Galileans, and with them Jesus and His disciples, reckoned from sunrise-to-sunrise while the Judeans reckoned from sunset-to-sunset.

OUTLINE OF THE PASSION WEEK

Due to the scope of these chapters, only a brief outline of the Passion Week can be given. It is an attempt to align the events with the days of the present calendar.

SATURDAY AND SUNDAY

In previous chapters of this book a suggested outline of Christ's life and ministry has been given. His last public ministry outside of Jerusalem was probably primarily in

---

[67]Morgenstern, *Hebrew Union College Annual*, X, 1-148; Stauffer, p. 95; Finkel, pp. 70-74; M. Black, "The Arrest and Trial of Jesus and the Date of the Last Supper," *New Testament Essays,* ed. by A. J. B. Higgins (Manchester, 1959), pp. 30-32.

Perea and Judea. A few days before the final Passover, Jesus drew near to Jerusalem (John 11:55), arriving at Bethany six days before the Passover (John 12:1), namely the Saturday before the Passion Week. That evening, Jesus was anointed at Simon the leper's house (Matt. 26:6-13; Mark 14:3-9; John 12:1-8).[68] On the next day (Sunday), there was a great crowd that came to Bethany to see Jesus (John 12:9-11).

MONDAY

The next day (John 12:12), Monday, was Jesus' triumphal entry into Jerusalem (Matt. 21:1-9; Mark 11:1-10; Luke 19:28-40; John 12:12-19), His visit to the temple (Matt. 21:10-11; Mark 11:11), and then His return to Bethany. The day of the triumphal entry would be Nisan 10 when the lamb was selected for Passover. Hence, the triumphal entry was the day when Christ presented Himself as Israel's Paschal lamb.

TUESDAY

On Tuesday on the way from Bethany to Jerusalem, Jesus cursed the fig tree (Matt. 21:18-19; Mark 11:12-14), and then He went to Jerusalem to cleanse the temple (Matt. 21:12-13; Mark 11:15-17; Luke 19:45-46). The religious leaders began to seek how they might destroy Him that evening, and that evening Jesus left Jerusalem, presumably returning to Bethany (Mark 11:18-19; Luke 19:47-48).

WEDNESDAY

On the way to Jerusalem on Wednesday, the disciples saw the withered fig tree (Matt. 21:20-22; Mark 11:20-26). At

[68]When one looks in the Matthean and Markan contexts (cf. Matt. 26:2; Mark 14:1), one notices that they mention two days rather than six days before the Passover. However, most commentators agree that the anointing should be dated six days before the Passover and that the story of the anointing in Bethany is inserted into Matthew (26:6-13) and Mark (14:3-9), and thus the time reference of two days in Matthew 26:2 and Mark 14:1 is not dating the anointing but the plot to seize Jesus. Cf. Alan Hugh M'Neile, *The Gospel according to St. Matthew* (London, 1915), p. 373; William Hendriksen, *Exposition of the Gospel according to Matthew* (Grand Rapids, 1973), p. 898; Taylor, *Mark*, p. 527; William L. Lane, *The Gospel according to Mark* (Grand Rapids, 1974), p. 492 n. 18.

the temple in Jerusalem, Jesus had a day of controversy with the religious leaders (Matt. 21:23 — 23:39; Mark 11:27 — 12:44; Luke 20:1 — 21:4). That afternoon Jesus went to the Mount of Olives and delivered the Olivet Discourse (Matt. 24:1 — 25:46; Mark 13:1-37; Luke 21:5-36). Two additional things occurred on that day: (1) Jesus predicted that in two days He would be crucified at the time of the Passover (Matt. 26:1-5; Mark 14:1-2; Luke 22:1-2); and (2) Judas planned the betrayal of Christ with the religious leaders (Matt. 26:14-16; Mark 14:10-11; Luke 22:3-6).

THURSDAY

On this day, He had His disciples prepare the Passover lamb (Matt. 26:17-19; Mark 14:12-16; Luke 22:7-13), and Jesus and His disciples had their Passover meal in the Upper Room (Matt. 26:20-30; Mark 14:17-26; Luke 22:14-30; John 13:1 — 14:31). Leaving the Upper Room, Jesus had a discourse with His disciples and offered an intercessory prayer in their behalf (Matt. 26:30-35; Mark 14:26-31; Luke 22:31-39; John 15:1 — 18:1). They arrived at the Garden of Gethsemane, and it was here where Jesus suffered in agony (Matt. 26:36-46; Mark 14:32-42; Luke 22:39-46; John 18:1). Later that night Jesus was betrayed and arrested (Matt. 26:47-56; Mark 14:43-52; Luke 22:47-53; John 18:2-12). During the rest of that night, Jesus was tried first by Annas and later by Caiaphas with the religious leaders (Matt. 26:57-75; Mark 14:53-72; Luke 22:54-65; John 18:13-27).

FRIDAY

Early in the morning, Jesus was tried by the Sanhedrin, Pilate, Herod Antipas, and Pilate again (Matt. 27:1-30; Mark 15:1-19; Luke 22:66 — 23:25; John 18:28 — 19:16). Jesus was then led to the cross and crucified at 9:00 a.m. and died at 3:00 p.m. and was buried later that day (Matt. 27:31-60; Mark 15:20-46; Luke 23:26-54; John 19:16-42). Christ the Paschal Lamb (1 Cor. 5:7) died at the time when the Israelites were sacrificing their Passover lambs.

SATURDAY

Jesus was lying in the tomb during the Sabbath, and the Pharisees secured Roman guards to keep watch of the tomb (Matt. 27:61-66; Mark 15:47; Luke 23:55-56).

SUNDAY

Christ was resurrected from the dead (Matt. 28:1-15; Mark 16:1-8[9-13]; Luke 24:1-35). He is a type of the offering of the first fruits which was offered the day after the Sabbath (Lev. 23:9-14; 1 Cor. 15:23).

CONCLUSION

The week of the Passion was filled with many events, beginning with the Saturday before the Passion Week and ending with the crucifixion of Christ on Friday and the resurrection on Sunday.

Chapter V

The Year of Christ's Crucifixion

The two greatest events in history were the crucifixion and the resurrection of our Lord. The Roman world judged Christ as an insignificant preacher in an insignificant land. By His Jewish contemporaries He was counted as a rabble-rouser espousing heretical teaching worthy of death. Yet His seemingly undistinguished death has become not only the bedrock of Christianity but also the most important death in history. It has become the touchstone of controversy in Christian and Jewish polemics. It seems strange, then, for such a significant historical event, that there continues to be discussion on the date of His crucifixion. One can pinpoint the date of the death of many world rulers, but the death of greatest renown is yet debated.

THE VARIETY OF THE DATES

In the discussion of this problem, various dates for the death of Christ have been proposed. They range from A.D. 21 to A.D. 36.

Eisler proposed that Jesus died in A.D. 21 for a violent messianic doctrine.[1] He based his theory upon the apocryphal work of the *Acts of Pilate*. The other extreme proposed

EDITOR'S NOTE: The essential content of this chapter was published in the book, *New Dimensions in New Testament Studies,* ed. by Richard N. Longenecker and Merrill C. Tenney, Grand Rapids: The Zondervan Corporation, 1974. Used by permission.
[1]Robert Eisler, ΙΗΣΟΥΣ ΒΑΣΙΛΕΥΣ ΟΥ ΒΑΣΙΛΕΥΣΑΣ (Heidelberg, 1929), I, xxxiii; II, 165, 254-70, 439-529; and the English condensed version *The Messiah Jesus and John the Baptist,* trans. by Alexander Haggerty Krappe (New York, 1931), pp. 16-20, 313, 363-70, 457-512.

by Keim,[2] followed by Lake[3] and Schonfield,[4] is that Christ died in the spring of A.D. 35 or 36. The adherents of this view feel that since the Jews believed that Aretas' (the Arab king of Petra) defeat of Antipas in A.D. 36 was divine revenge for Antipas' beheading of John the Baptist,[5] John's death and the death of Jesus must be placed as close as possible to the year A.D. 36.

Between A.D. 21 and 36 there are advocates for nearly every year. Only the more prominent dates with some of their adherents are here listed. Meyer[6] and King[7] argue for A.D. 27; Winter A.D. 28;[8] Turner,[9] Loisy,[10] and Hölscher[11] A.D. 29; Olmstead,[12] Blinzler,[13] Madison,[14] Ruckstuhl,[15]

[2]Theodor Keim, *The History of Jesus of Nazara,* trans. by Arthur Ransom, IV (London, 1879), 222-23 n. 2; VI (London, 1883), 234-44.
[3]Kirsopp Lake, "The Date of Herod's Marriage with Herodias, and the Chronology of the Gospels," *The Expositor,* 8th series, IV (November, 1912), 462-77.
[4]Hugh J. Schonfield, *The Jesus Party* (New York, 1974), pp. 46-47, 51-53, 305.
[5]Jos. *Ant.* xviii. 5. 1-2 §§ 113-17.
[6]Eduard Meyer, *Ursprung und Anfänge des Christentums* (Stuttgart and Berlin, 1923), III, 171.
[7]Charles King, "The Outlines of New Testament Chronology," *Catholic Biblical Quarterly,* CCLXXVIII (January-March, 1945), 145-47, 153.
[8]Paul Winter, *On the Trial of Jesus,* Vol. I of *Studia Judaica* (Berlin, 1961), p. 175 n. 5.
[9]Cuthbert Hamilton Turner, "Chronology of the New Testament," *A Dictionary of the Bible,* ed. by James Hastings, *et al.,* I (1898), 411-15.
[10]Alfred Loisy, *Les Évangiles Synoptiques* (Paris, 1907-8), I, 386-89; II, 490.
[11]Gustav Hölscher, "Die Hohenpriesterliste bei Josephus und die evangelische Chronologie," *Sitzungsberichte der Heidelberger Akadamie der Wissenschaften — Philosophisch-historische Klasse,* XXX (Heidelberg, 1940), 26.
[12]A. T. Olmstead, *Jesus in the Light of History* (New York, 1942), pp. 279-81.
[13]Josef Blinzler, *The Trial of Jesus,* trans. by Isabel and Florence McHugh (2nd ed.; Westminster, MD, 1959), pp. 72-80.
[14]Leslie P. Madison, "Problems of Chronology in the Life of Christ" (unpublished Th.D. dissertation, Dallas Theological Seminary, 1963), pp. 149-63.
[15]Eugen Ruckstuhl, *Chronology of the Last Days of Jesus,* trans. by Victor J. Drapela (New York, 1965), pp. 1-12.

and Jeremias[16] A.D. 30; Anderson,[17] Bammel,[18] and Stauffer[19] A.D. 32; and Fotheringham,[20] Ogg,[21] Maier,[22] and Reicke[23] A.D. 33. Thus one sees there is great diversity. The task now is to limit these options and come to a date that best fits the evidence.

THE LIMITATION OF THE DATE

There are certain lines of evidence from sacred and secular history which limit the possibilities for the crucifixion date.

THE OFFICIALS OF THE CRUCIFIXION

Caiaphas. The Gospels (Matt. 26:3, 57; John 11:49-53; 18:13-14) explicitly have Caiaphas as the high priest involved in the trial of Jesus. He was the high priest from A.D. 18[24] to the Passover of A.D. 37.[25] Thus the crucifixion must have occurred sometime between A.D. 18 and the Passover of A.D. 36 since Caiaphas was deposed at the Passover of 37.

Pilate. The Gospels (Matt. 27:2-26; Mark 15:1-15; Luke 23:1-25; John 18:28 — 19:16), as well as Acts (4:27) and

[16]Joachim Jeremias, *The Eucharistic Words of Jesus,* trans. by Norman Perrin (3rd ed.; London, 1966), pp. 36-41.
[17]Robert Anderson, *The Coming Prince* (5th ed.; London, 1895), pp. 97-105.
[18]Ernst Bammel, "Φίλος τοῦ Καίσαρος, " *Theologische Literaturzeitung,* LXXVII (April, 1952), 205-10.
[19]Ethelbert Stauffer, *Jesus and His Story,* trans. by Dorothea M. Barton (London, 1960), pp. 91-110.
[20]J. K. Fotheringham, "The Evidence of Astronomy and Technical Chronology," *The Journal of Theological Studies,* XXXV (April, 1934), 142-62.
[21]George Ogg, *The Chronology of the Public Ministry of Jesus* (Cambridge, 1940), pp. 244-77.
[22]Paul L. Maier, "Sejanus, Pilate, and the Date of the Crucifixion," *Church History,* XXXVII (March, 1968), 3-13.
[23]Bo Reicke, *The New Testament Era,* trans. by David E. Green (Philadelphia, 1968), pp. 183-84.
[24]Jos. *Ant.* xviii. 2. 2 § 35.
[25]Jos. *Ant.* xviii. 4. 3 §§ 90-95; Harold W. Hoehner, *Herod Antipas* (Cambridge, 1972), Appendix VIII, pp. 313-16.

a pastoral epistle (1 Tim. 6:13), attest that Jesus was tried by the Prefect Pontius Pilate. The tenure of Pilate's rule in Judea is outlined by Josephus. First, since his predecessor Valerius Gratus held office for eleven years,[26] all of which fell within Tiberius' reign (A.D. 14-37), Pilate's reign could not have begun before A.D. 25. Second, Josephus states that Pilate ruled for ten years and that Tiberius died before Pilate reached Rome.[27] It is most likely that he left Judea in the winter of A.D. 36/37.[28] Therefore, Pilate's reign would have been the ten-year period from A.D. 26 to 36 and Christ's crucifixion must have been between these dates.

Conclusion. Having set the limits of the two officials of Christ's trial, Christ's crucifixion must have occurred sometime between the years of A.D. 26 and 36. This, therefore, eliminates the A.D. 21 date proposed by Eisler based upon the apocryphal *Acts of Pilate* (which Eusebius did not consider credible[29]) published by the Emperor Maximinus in A.D. 311. Eisler's theory makes havoc of the chronology of Josephus, and numismatic evidence supports Josephus' chronology.[30] Eisler's view also makes havoc of the chronology of the Bible, for Luke 3:1-2 states that the commencement of John the Baptist's ministry was in Tiberius' fifteenth year, that is, A.D. 28/29. This means that John's ministry began eight years after Jesus' death! The many textual emendations Eisler makes to support his theory render it immediately suspect.[31]

Thus the crucifixion occurred between A.D. 26 and 36.

THE DAY OF THE CRUCIFIXION

Having already discussed this in more detail in the previous chapter, one need not go into detail here. Suffice it to

[26]Jos. *Ant.* xviii. 2. 2 § 35.
[27]Jos. *Ant.* xviii. 4. 2 § 89.
[28]Hoehner, *Herod Antipas,* pp. 313-16.
[29]Eusebius *Historia Ecclesiastica* i. 9. 3.
[30]Cf. P. L. Hedley, "Pilate's Arrival in Judaea," *The Journal of Theological Studies,* XXXV (January, 1934), 57; Ethelbert Stauffer, "Zur Münzprägung und Judenpolitik des Pontius Pilatus," *La Nouvelle Clio,* I/II (Octobre, 1950), 495-514, esp. 506-9.
[31]For a fuller discussion, see Ogg, *Chronology,* pp. 282-85.

say it was concluded that Jesus died on Friday, Nisan 14, at 3 p.m. This means that Christ died when many Jews were slaying their paschal lambs which according to Josephus was from the ninth to the eleventh hour, that is, from three to five p.m.[32] According to Paul (1 Cor. 5:7) Christ is portrayed as "our paschal lamb [who] has been sacrificed."[33]

One must now determine which year between the extremes of A.D. 26 and A.D. 36 is the most plausible as the year of Christ's crucifixion.

THE CONTRIBUTION OF ASTRONOMY

Having concluded that Jesus died on a Friday and on Nisan 14, one must determine in which years within the previously established limits of A.D. 26-36 Nisan 14 fell on Friday.

The Jewish month was a lunar month having no less than twenty-nine and no more than thirty days. The first day of the month was determined from the new moon. Of course, the new moon is not visible, but one or two days after the new moon, a faintly glowing moon sickle appears. When two trustworthy witnesses informed the priestly calendar commission, under oath, that they had seen the new moon, the day would be declared the first of the new month. When there was a problem of visibility, the commencement of the new month could not be postponed for more than a day. Because of new data from various calendars as well as an advancement in astronomical knowledge, one is able to determine within minutes the new moon of the Jewish calendar at the time of Christ. Astronomers can determine the days of the week on which Nisan 14 fell in Christ's time with great certainty.

There have been several studies in this, and their conclusions are that the only possible times Nisan 14 fell on

---

[32]Jos. *BJ* vi. 9. 3 § 423.
[33]This is also supported by Gospel of Peter 3; Babylonian Talmud: Sanhedrin 43*a*.

Friday were in the years of A.D. 27, 30, 33, and 36.[34] Of these, A.D. 27 is the least likely astronomically. In that year it is probable that Nisan 14 fell on Thursday rather than Friday. The year of A.D. 30 has also been debated, but it is reasonably certain that Nisan 14 was a Friday that year.[35]

In conclusion, then, the calculations of astronomers would limit the probable years of Christ's crucifixion on Friday, Nisan 14, to the years 30, 33, and 36, with A.D. 27 as an unlikely possibility.

THE MINISTRY OF CHRIST

Having limited the crucifixion date to the years of A.D. 30, 33, 36, and possibly 27, it is now appropriate to discuss how these years concur with the ministry of Christ. First to be considered is the A.D. 27 date. To deal with this, one must look at the commencement of Christ's ministry. Having gone into more detail on this subject in another chapter,[36] only the results relevant to the present problem will be stated. Luke 3:1-2 indicates that John the Baptist's ministry started in Tiberius' fifteenth year which was A.D. 28/29. Jesus' ministry followed this and therefore the A.D. 27 date is not only questionable astronomically but is impossible biblically — if one takes Luke 3:1-2 seriously. This is confirmed in John 2:20 where at the first Passover of Christ's ministry He speaks of the temple edifice having stood for forty-six years. Since it was completed in 18/17 B.C., forty-six years later would bring the date to the year A.D. 29/30. Therefore, the A.D. 27 date is not a viable option for Christ's crucifixion.

---

[34]Cf. J. K. Fotheringham, "Astronomical Evidence for the Date of the Crucifixion," *The Journal of Theological Studies,* XII (October, 1910), 120-27; Fotheringham, *The Journal of Theological Studies,* XXXV, 152-62; Ogg, *Chronology,* pp. 261-77; Jeremias, *Eucharistic Words,* pp. 36-41; George Ogg, "The Chronology of the Last Supper," *Historicity and Chronology of the New Testament* (London, 1965), pp. 92-96.

[35]Jeremias, *Eucharistic Words,* pp. 39-40. A new work containing the computer print-out of the occurrences of the new moons further questions that Nisan 14 in A.D. 30 occurred on Friday. According to the computers Nisan 14 in A.D. 30 occurred on Thursday. See Herman H. Goldstine, *New and Full Moons, 1001 B.C. to A.D. 1651* (Philadelphia, 1973), p. 86.

[36]See Chapter II.

Second, in considering the other extreme, the A.D. 36
date, one sees that Luke 3:1 also makes shipwreck of this
late date. There is no indication in the Gospels that Jesus'
ministry lasted six years. The adherents of this late date, as
mentioned above, base it on the supposition that John the
Baptist was not beheaded until shortly before A.D. 36. According to Josephus, the Jews attributed Herod Antipas'
defeat by Aretas in A.D. 36 to revenge by God for the
beheading of John.[37] Those who hold this view think that
Josephus implies that Herod Antipas' defeat occurred not
long after he had beheaded John. It is important to note that
the reason for John's beheading was that Herodias did not
like his interference in their affairs. In marrying Herodias,
Herod Antipas got rid of his first wife who was Aretas'
daughter. Accordingly, it is thought that Aretas' retaliation
would have occurred soon after his daughter returned home.
Josephus clearly indicates, however, that the divorce was
the beginning of hostilities[38] and that other incidents such as
the boundary disputes finally led to war.[39] Certainly Aretas
would have waited for the most opportune time, and that was
in A.D. 36, shortly after the time when the Romans had been
engaged in a struggle against Artabanus III, king of Parthia.
At that time Aretas would have had little fear of defeat.[40] So
it is not necessary to see an immediate revenge by Aretas
and thus John's death need not be sometime near A.D. 36.

Therefore, this late date for the crucifixion based on an
inference from Josephus that John the Baptist's death must
have occurred very shortly before the time of Herod
Antipas' defeat by Aretas, is only an inference and nothing
more. This theory makes havoc of the Gospels' chronology,
whereas if one follows the Gospels' chronological framework one can fit in the events in Josephus very easily. It is

[37]Jos. *Ant.* xviii. 5. 2 §§ 116-19.
[38]Jos. *Ant.* xviii. 5. 1 § 113.
[39]Emil Schürer, *The History of the Jewish People in the Age of Jesus
Christ*, new English version rev. and ed. by Geza Vermes, Fergus Millar,
and Matthew Black (Edinburgh, 1973), I, 350.
[40]Cf. Hoehner, *Herod Antipas,* pp. 251-57.

better to base one's chronology on the Gospels than on what in effect is *only* an inference from Josephus. Hence, the A.D. 36 date for crucifixion is unacceptable.

This leaves only two plausible dates for the crucifixion, namely, A.D. 30 and 33. There are a great number of scholars who hold to A.D. 30 as the date of Christ's crucifixion. However, if one accepts John's ministry beginning in Tiberius' fifteenth year, A.D. 28/29 (Luke 3:1-2), then Christ would have had a ministry of only about one year. There are those who followed Ramsay by stating that one must reckon from the time of the decree when Tiberius become co-regent with Augustus.[41] This would make the commencement of John's ministry around A.D. 25/26 and Jesus' ministry shortly thereafter. This view is untenable for the following two reasons. First, there is no evidence, either from historical documents or coins, that Tiberius' reign was ever reckoned from his co-regency. On the contrary his reign is always reckoned from the time he became sole ruler after Augustus' death on August 19, A.D. 14.[42] Second, those who accept this theory are not in agreement as to the beginning of the co-regency. Therefore, other scholars who hold to the A.D. 30 crucifixion, such as Blinzler,[43] feel that one must reckon according to Syrian chronology — especially since Luke was born in Syria, where Tiberius' first year would be from August 19, A.D. 14 to Tishri 1 (September/October) and therefore the fifteenth year would be Tishri 1, A.D. 27 to Tishri 1, 28. John the Baptist's ministry began then, and Christ's ministry followed shortly thereafter. But is one sure that Luke reckoned in this manner, especially since he was writing to Theophilus, a Roman official? It would seem that he would have used a Roman system, reckoning either from Tiberius' accession date or the Julian calendar.[44] Blinzler feels that A.D. 28 as marking the commencement of Christ's

[41]W. M. Ramsay, *Was Christ Born at Bethlehem?* (2nd ed.; London, 1898), pp. 199-200, 221.
[42]Many examples could be cited but see chapter II esp. nn. 11-13 and Ogg, pp. 174-83.
[43]Blinzler, *Trial of Jesus*, p. 73.
[44]See further discussion in chapter II.

ministry is substantiated by John 2:20 where the Jews state that the temple had been in continuous construction for forty-six years since Herod began to build it in 20/19 B.C.[45] But the Jews are talking about the temple edifice ὁ ναός which was completed in 18/17 B.C. as having stood for forty-six years, that is, the Passover of A.D. 30, rather than the temple precincts τὸ ἱερόν which were still in the building process.[46] Finally, Blinzler states that with this reckoning Christ had a ministry of two years and some months. Although John mentions in his Gospel only three Passovers (John 2:13; 6:4; 11:55), it is thought by some that Christ's ministry need not be more than two years. However, this view ignores the time note in John 4:35 and does not adequately explain the chronological setting for the un-named feast of John 5:1.[47] In addition this view requires a transposition of chapters 5 and 6 of John's Gospel. A three year and some months ministry of Christ better explains the evidence.

In conclusion, the A.D. 30 crucifixion is not the best possibility because: (1) it has some (not great) difficulty astronomically; (2) it has difficulty in fitting Luke 3:1-2 into Christ's life unless one reckons according to the Syrian chronology which one is not at all sure Luke was using; (3) it attempts to explain John 2:20 as referring to Herod's rebuild-ing the temple precincts when actually the passage is talking about the temple edifice; and (4) it limits Christ's ministry to a little over two years which requires a transposition of John 5 and 6 and does not explain the time note of John 4:35 or the unnamed feast of John 5:1.

This leaves only A.D. 33 as the most plausible date for the crucifixion. First, it is sound astronomically.[48] Second, it is not limited to one dating system for reckoning the com-mencement of the Baptist's ministry in Tiberius' fifteenth year (Luke 3:1-2). Although this author prefers to date the

[45]Blinzler, *Trial of Jesus,* p. 74.
[46]See chapter II.
[47]For a discussion of this, see Ogg, *Chronology,* pp. 1-149, 289-304.
[48]This has been recently confirmed by Goldstine, p. 87.

beginning of John's ministry from the accession of Tiberius or by the Julian calendar which results in A.D. 28/29 as marking the beginning of John's ministry, the other systems could be utilized depending on how long John ministered before Jesus began His ministry. Third, it allows for a ministry of more than three years beginning in the summer or autumn of A.D. 29 and ending at the Passover of A.D. 33. Fourth, it adequately explains John 2:20 as the temple edifice which had stood for forty-six years since it was completed, so that the Passover of A.D. 30 was Christ's first Passover of His ministry. Fifth, there is no need of transposition of chapters 5 and 6 of the Gospel of John.

There are two objections that are raised against the A.D. 33 crucifixion date. First, the most prevalent one, is that one cannot have the crucifixion so late because it would interfere with the date of Paul's conversion and the apostolic age.[49] However, one could reverse this question and ask if Paul's conversion is placed too early in the objector's scheme.[50] In the end one does not determine the chronology of the Gospels on the basis of the chronology of the apostolic age or vice versa.

The second objection raised is that with the A.D. 30 crucifixion, Jesus began His ministry in A.D. 27/28 and He would have been only thirty or thirty-one years of age if one assumes that He was born in the winter of 5/4 B.C. This fits well with Luke 3:23. Luke's statement that Christ was "about thirty years of age," however, is elastic. Assuming His birth to have been in the winter of 5/4 B.C. and the commencement of His ministry in the summer or autumn of A.D. 29, He would have been thirty-two years of age with his

[49]Jeremias, *Eucharistic Words,* p. 39 n. 1; G. B. Caird, "The Chronology of the NT," *The Interpreter's Dictionary of the Bible,* ed. by George Arthur Buttrick, *et al.,* I (1962), 603. Cf. also Werner Georg Kümmel, *Introduction to the New Testament,* trans. by Howard Clark Kee (17th rev. ed., Nashville, 1975), pp. 252-55.

[50]In fact the present author worked on Paul's chronology assuming the A.D. 30 crucifixion date with the result of having Paul's conversion date in A.D. 35, cf. Harold Hoehner, "Chronology of the Apostolic Age" (unpublished Th.D. dissertation, Dallas Theological Seminary, 1965), pp. 154-56, 200-204, 381.

thirty-third birthday approaching in the winter of A.D. 29/30. This is in keeping with the tenor of Luke 3:23 and the objection is not weighty enough to be a serious obstacle. Both of these objections are easily answered and do not detract from the soundness of the A.D. 33 date for Christ's crucifixion.

In conclusion, the A.D. 33 crucifixion date best fits the evidence of astronomy and the chronological aspects of the life of Christ.

THE CONTRIBUTION OF HISTORY

The conclusion up to this point is that A.D. 33 is the best date for the crucifixion of Christ. Interestingly enough, secular history not only agrees with this conclusion, but confirms it as the most well-grounded date.

In the trial of Jesus, Pilate is pictured as one who was submissive to the pressures of the Jews who were demanding that he hand Jesus over to them whereas he is described by his contemporary Philo[51] and later by Josephus[52] as being one who was greedy, inflexible, and cruel, and who resorted to robbery and oppression. This great difference between the biblical narrative on the one hand and Philo and Josephus on the other hand can be explained.

It is probable that when Pilate succeeded Valerius Gratus as prefect in Judea in A.D. 26 he was appointed by the equestrian Lucius Aelius Sejanus. This Sejanus had gained one of the two highest positions an equestrian was able to attain, namely, the prefect of the Praetorian Guard which was the elite corps of 9000 soldiers of the imperial palace. But beyond this, by A.D. 26 or 27 when Tiberius retired to the island of Capri, Sejanus was virtually in full control of the government.[53] Sejanus was a dedicated anti-Semite[54] who wanted to exterminate the Jewish race.[55]

[51]Philo *Legatio ad Gaium* 301-2 [hereafter Philo *Leg.*].
[52]Jos. *Ant.* xviii. 3. 1 §§ 55-59; *BJ* ii. 9. 2-4 §§ 169-77.
[53]Tacitus *Annales* iv. 41, 57, 67 [hereafter Tac. *Ann.*]; Dio lviii. 1; Suetonius *Tiberius* xxxix-xli [hereafter Suet. *Tib.*] cf. Frank Burr Marsh, *The Reign of Tiberius* (London, 1931), pp. 181-83.
[54]Philo *In Flaccum* 1.
[55]Philo *Leg.* 159-61.

Apparently Pilate implemented Sejanus' anti-Jewish policy in Judea.[56] Almost immediately after his arrival in Judea in A.D. 26[57] Pilate introduced Roman standards with the embossed figures of the emperor into Jerusalem.[58] The Jews' indignation was aroused and as a result they sent a delegation to Caesarea to plead for their removal.[59] Finally, after five days of demonstration, Pilate realized that the Jews would rather die than violate their laws. When confronted with this situation, Pilate ordered the removal of the standards that had caused them to react so vehemently.

Josephus' second recorded conflict between Pilate and the Jews was when he seized funds from the Corbanus, the temple treasury, for constructing an aqueduct in

[56]For further discussion of Pilate's rule, see Hoehner, *Herod Antipas,* pp. 172-83.

[57]Josephus (*Ant.* xviii. 3. 1 § 55) states that the troops were going to their winter quarters in Jerusalem. If *Megillat Taanit* ix (for text and discussion, see Solomon Zeitlin, "Megillat Taanit as a Source for Jewish Chronology and History in the Hellenistic and Roman Periods," *The Jewish Quarterly Review,* X [October, 1919 and January, 1920], 239, 241, 259-61) is speaking of the same incident, it means that the standards were removed on Chislev 3. According to Parker and Dubberstein, Chislev 3 would have been December 2, A.D. 26, Richard A. Parker and Waldo H. Dubberstein, *Babylonian Chronology 626 B.C. — A.D. 75* (2nd ed.; Providence, 1956), p. 46.

[58]Jos. *Ant.* xviii. 3. 1 §§ 55-59; *BJ* ii. 9. 2-3 §§ 169-74; cf. Carl H. Kraeling, "The Episode of the Roman Standards at Jerusalem," *The Harvard Theological Review,* XXXV (October, 1942), 263-89.

[59]Apparently it was not the standards *per se* but the embossed figures of the emperor (προτομὰς Καίσαρος) that bothered the Jews (Jos. *Ant.* xviii. 3. 1 § 55; cf. *BJ* ii. 9. 2 § 169). The Jews had allowed other rulers to bring standards without images into Jerusalem (Jos. *Ant.* xviii. 3. 1 § 56). Also according to Jos. *Ant.* xviii. 3. 1 § 59, the εἰόνες were removed from Jerusalem (though Jos. *BJ* ii. 9. 3 § 174 the σημαῖαι were removed). It seems that the Jews objected in this case on the basis of a rigid interpretation of their Law against the making of images (cf. Exod. 20:4; Deut. 4:16; cf. also J.-B. Frey, "La question des images chez les Juifs. A la lumière des récentes découvertes," *Biblica,* XV, Fasc. 2 and 3 [1934], 273-82. Specifically the prohibition was against the production or use of any representation of men or animals, cf. E. Bevan, *Holy Images* [London, 1940], pp. 48-49; Edwin R. Goodenough, *Jewish Symbols in Greco-Roman Period,* IV [New York, 1954], 11-24).

Jerusalem.[60] Later when Pilate visited Jerusalem, the Jews besieged him with angry clamor and he, realizing the possibility of an uprising, instructed his soldiers to mingle among the crowd dressed as civilians armed with hidden clubs. When the protest became more pronounced the soldiers, on a pre-arranged signal, drew the clubs from under their tunics and began to beat them, killing many.[61]

In Luke 13:1 some people came to Jesus[62] and told Him of the Galileans whose blood Pilate had mingled with their sacrifices. It has been suggested that the story was fabricated by those reporting it to Jesus,[63] but there is no convincing reason to doubt its authenticity.[64] Surely this portrayal of Pilate in the biblical narrative is in keeping with that in Josephus and Philo. Although it is not possible to know exactly when it occurred, certainly it was during Christ's ministry, probably at one of the great Jewish festivals (possibly the Passover of A.D. 32) when the Galileans would have been in Jerusalem. This incident would only make for enmity between Pilate and the Galilean tetrarch, Herod Antipas.

Finally, since the standards affair failed, Pilate issued

---

[60]Jos. *BJ* ii. 9. 4 §§ 175-77; *Ant.* xviii. 3. 2 §§ 60-62. With regard to this treasury, Zeitlin states: "The money in this treasury was not in the same category as the communal money of the Temple, but was considered private property held as a religious trust. It consisted of the sums deposited by the Nazarites for their sacrifices and was not used for any other purpose." Solomon Zeitlin, *The Rise and Fall of the Judaean State,* I (Philadephia, 1967), 143.

[61]Eusebius *Historia Ecclesiasticus* ii. 6-7 quotes Jos. *BJ* ii. 9. 4 §§ 175-77 verbatim, except an alteration in the length of the aqueduct.

[62]The words παρῆσαν δέ τινες are better translated "they came" or "they had come" rather than "they were present," cf. Alfred Plummer, *A Critical and Exegetical Commentary on the Gospel according to S. Luke* (4th ed.; Edinburgh, 1905), pp. 337-38; John Martin Creed, *The Gospel according to St. Luke* (London, 1930), p. 180; Josef Blinzler, "Die Niedermetzelung von Galiläern durch Pilatus," *Novum Testamentum,* II (January, 1957), 25 n. 2.

[63]For a brief discussion of this see, T. W. Manson, *The Sayings of Jesus* (London, 1949), p. 65.

[64]Cf. C. H. Dodd, *The Parables of the Kingdom* (3rd ed.; London, 1936), p. 65; Blinzler, *Trial of Jesus,* p. 179; Winter, *Trial of Jesus,* p. 176 n. 9.

offensive coins, a crosier symbolizing the Roman emperor worship, in A.D. 29/30 for purposes of indoctrination.[65]

How could all these insults continue without the protest of the Jews to the Roman government? This was not a problem as long as Sejanus was in full control. Any complaint sent to Tiberius would be destroyed by Sejanus before it reached the island of Capri.[66] Sejanus was making every effort to gain more power, possibly to become emperor himself. He even poisoned Tiberius' son Drusus in A.D. 23.[67] Tiberius was so mesmerized by Sejanus that he did not suspect him of the murder. With the removal of Drusus, Tiberius considered the sons of Germanicus (a nephew of Tiberius who died in A.D. 19) as his successors[68] but Sejanus disposed of Germanicus' wife, Agrippina, and her two oldest sons — only Gaius survived because Sejanus fell before he was able to get rid of him.[69]

Sejanus was rising to even greater heights, and in A.D. 29 the Senate voted that his birthday should be publicly observed.[70] By A.D. 30 he was so influential that senators and other high officials looked upon him as if he were actually the emperor.[71] Finally Tiberius' suspicions were aroused and he secretly appointed Naevius Sertorius Macro as prefect of the Praetorian Guard and sent him to Rome to overthrow Sejanus. Macro tricked Sejanus by confirming a rumor that Tiberius was going to grant him the *tribunicia potestas* — supreme authority over Roman civil affairs. Sejanus, overjoyed with the announcement, rushed into the Senate. Macro took control of the Praetorian Guard while the letter from Tiberius was read in the Senate and Sejanus

---

[65]Stauffer, *La Nouvelle Clio,* I/II, 495-514, esp. 506-8; Ethelbert Stauffer, *Jerusalem und Rom* (Bern and München, 1957), pp. 17, 134 n. 7.
[66]Tac. *Ann.* iv. 41.
[67]Tac. *Ann.* iv. 8; Suet. *Tib.* lxii. 1; Dio lvii. 22. 1-4.
[68]For a discussion of the bitter party struggles in Rome at that time, see Frank Burr Marsh, "Roman Parties in the Reign of Tiberius," *The American Historical Review,* XXXI (January, 1926), 233-50.
[69]Tac. *Ann.* vi. 3-4; Suet. *Tib.* lxv.
[70]Dio lviii. 2. 7-8; Suet. *Tib.* lxv.
[71]Dio lviii. 4. 1.

was denounced. On that day, October 18, A.D. 31, Sejanus was executed.[72]

This, no doubt, caused immediate tremors throughout the Empire, especially to those who were appointed by Sejanus. Tiberius had been anti-Semitic (possibly influenced by Sejanus), as seen by his expulsion of the Jews from Rome in A.D. 19,[73] but now he was more favorable toward them. According to Philo, it now became obvious to Tiberius that the charges brought against the Jews were unfounded, having been fabricated by Sejanus. Consequently he ordered the governors (many of whom were probably appointed by Sejanus) throughout the Empire not to mistreat the Jews.[74] This order had its effect in Judea. Early in A.D. 32 Pilate stopped issuing coins that were offensive to the Jews.[75]

Philo records an incident where Pilate set up in the former palace of Herod the Great gilded votive shields bearing the name, though not the image, of the emperor. When Pilate refused to hear the Jews' request for their removal, some prominent Jews, including the four sons of Herod, appealed to the Emperor Tiberius. Tiberius expressed the strongest disapproval of Pilate's action and ordered him to take down the shields and to have them transferred to the temple of Augustus at Caesarea.[76]

There are three observations that should be noted. First, it seems strange that the Jews were offended at these aniconic shields unless, as Brandon suggests, the inscription on them may have contained some reference to the divinity of the emperor.[77] Second, one can only guess who the four

---

[72]Dio lviii. 9-12; Tac. *Ann.* vi. 48; Suet. *Tib.* lxv; Jos. *Ant.* xviii. 6. 6 §§ 181-82.
[73]Jos. *Ant.* xviii. 3. 5 §§ 81-85; Suet. *Tib.* xxxvi; Dio lvi. 18. *5a;* Tac. *Ann.* ii. 85; E. Mary Smallwood, "Some Notes on the Jews under Tiberius," *Latomus,* XV (Juillet-Septembre, 1956), 314-29.
[74]Philo *Leg.* 159-61.
[75]E. Bammel, "Syrian Coinage and Pilate," *The Journal of Jewish Studies,* II, No. 2 (1951), 108-10.
[76]Philo *Leg.* 299-305. For a recent discussion of this episode, see Paul L. Maier, "The Episode of the Golden Roman Shields at Jerusalem," *The Harvard Theological Review,* LXII (January, 1969), 109-21.
[77]S. G. F. Brandon, *Jesus and the Zealots* (Manchester, 1967), p. 74.

sons of Herod were, but certainly Herod Antipas and Philip the Tetrarch were among them and possibly the other two were Herod (Philip), who resided in Palestine, and Agrippa I, Herodias' brother. One important factor to remember is that Herod Antipas also had been a friend of the deceased Sejanus[78] and wanted at this time to prove his loyalty to Tiberius. Third, although the identity of this episode has been disputed,[79] it occurred later in Pilate's administration because: (1) the reference to Pilate's fear of impeachment implies it; (2) the fact that the Jewish embassy was able to report to Tiberius directly; and (3) the fact that Pilate and Antipas, both friends of Sejanus, were opposing each other may also indicate that this event occurred after Sejanus' death. So long as Sejanus was in power Pilate had nothing to fear. Since the Herodian brothers were there, it probably occurred at a Jewish festival, possibly the Feast of Tabernacles of A.D. 32.[80]

Why then did Pilate set up the shields when his position was so precarious? It is possible that he wanted to dissociate himself from Sejanus and ingratiate himself to Tiberius by promoting emperor worship. But it backfired. In fact the Jews stated that disrespect for the Jewish Law brings no honor to Tiberius.[81] Also, it presented an opportunity for Herod Antipas to put his foot forward in dissociating himself from Sejanus and to gain the favor of Tiberius. Once before Herod Antipas had been at odds with Pilate when the latter mixed the blood of the Galileans with their sacrifices (Luke 13:1). Now with the shields incident Herod Antipas could report of Pilate's Sejanian anti-Semitic attitude to Tiberius. Their enmity is mentioned in Luke 23:12.

In conclusion, with the death of Sejanus and the unsuccessful attempt of Pilate to ingratiate himself with the emperor, one can readily see that Pilate was a man with a broken backbone. This is exactly how the Gospels portray

---

[78]Jos. *Ant.* xviii. 7. 2 § 250.
[79]Cf. A. D. Doyle, "Pilate's Career and the Date of the Crucifixion," *The Journal of Theological Studies,* XLII (October, 1941), 190-93.
[80]Hoehner, *Herod Antipas,* pp. 180-81.
[81]Philo *Leg.* 299, 301.

him in the trial of Christ. Hence only the A.D. 33 date for the crucifixion makes sense. Pilate was an inflexible and ruthless character as long as his mentor Sejanus was in power. But with Christ's trial in A.D. 33 he appears submissive. Although he realized that Jesus was innocent and ought to be released, the Jews cried out that if he released Jesus he was not a friend of Caesar (John 19:12). The reverse implication is that he was still a friend of Sejanus and/or friendly toward his policies. The phrase "friend of Caesar" is a technical phrase which meant that such a one was among the elite in the Roman government who were loyal to the emperor.[82] To lose the status of *amici Caesaris* meant political doom. Pilate realized that he had overstepped himself in the shields episode and could not afford to get into more trouble with Tiberius. Moreover, if Pilate had just received the instructions from Tiberius to remove the shields, the Jews would have only recently learned of their success and Pilate would have known all too well that he could not afford to quarrel with the emperor.

Thus, the A.D. 33 date for the death of Christ best explains the evidence of both sacred and secular history.

The Significance of the Date

The A.D. 33 crucifixion date is significant to the interpretation of the New Testament in at least three areas. All of these confirm the A.D. 33 date.

PILATE'S CHANGE OF ATTITUDE

Brandon thinks that the characterization of Pilate in the Gospels as being a weak, abject figure as opposed to that given in Josephus and Philo is ludicrous.[83] Brandon says that Mark is writing an apologetic to explain away Pilate's responsibility for Christ's death and place that responsibility on the Jews. Brandon also argues that the Gospels' picture of

[82]Cf. an interesting study on this phrase, Bammel, *Theologische Literaturzeitung*, LXXVII, 205-10; John Crook, *Concilium Principis* (Cambridge, 1955), pp. 21-30.
[83]S. G. F. Brandon, *The Trial of Jesus of Nazareth* (London, 1968), pp. 99, 190 n. 100; cf. also pp. 35-41; Brandon, *Jesus*, pp. 68-80, 248.

Pilate's attempt to save Jesus and his yielding to the pressures of the Jews is inaccurate in light of the remarks in Josephus and Philo indicating how inflexible and contemptuous he was toward the Jews.[84]

Along similar lines of argumentation, Wilson contends that in the light of Josephus and Philo the Gospels give a distorted portrait of Pilate.[85]

However, both Brandon[86] and Wilson[87] assume the A.D. 30 date for the crucifixion and if they would accept the A.D. 33 date then the characterization of Pilate given in the Gospels is indeed very intelligible.

In the end the A.D. 33 date for Christ's death satisfactorily explains the change of Pilate's attitude toward the Jews and prevents one from judging the biblical portrayal of him as being inaccurate. The Gospels do not contradict Josephus and Philo with regard to Pilate, but rather complement these sources.

FRIEND OF CAESAR

In John 19:12 the Jews state that if Pilate does not release Jesus to them he is not a friend of Caesar. The status of being a friend of Caesar was indeed prestigious and if the crucifixion occurred in A.D. 30 the Jews' threat would be empty indeed since Tiberius could not be reached except through Sejanus. However, in A.D. 33 this is a loaded threat. Pilate had just received instructions from Tiberius to remove the shields from Jerusalem. After the death of Sejanus, Tiberius' new policy was not to disturb the Jewish customs and institutions.[88]

Thus the A.D. 33 date for Christ's death fits well in this scriptural context because it fills the threat by the Jews with meaning.

[84]Brandon, *Jesus*, pp. 253-64, 363-64; *Trial*, pp. 35-44, 75-76, 81-139.
[85]William Riley Wilson, *The Execution of Jesus* (New York, 1970), pp. 17-23, 131-34.
[86]Brandon, *Trial*, pp. 146, 150.
[87]Wilson, p. 1.
[88]Philo *Leg.* 161, 304-5.

FRIENDSHIP OF PILATE AND HEROD ANTIPAS

There was enmity between Pilate and Herod Antipas because Pilate mixed the blood of the Galileans with their sacrifices (Luke 13:1 — probably at the Passover of A.D. 32) and because of the shields episode (probably at the Feast of Tabernacles of A.D. 32) recorded in Philo. Both had been friends of Sejanus, but now after Sejanus' death they wanted to dissociate themselves from Sejanus and gain the favorable acceptance of Tiberius. Each was willing to do this at the expense of the other.

The shields incident backfired for Pilate. Herod Antipas reported the episode to Tiberius at the expense of Pilate and for his own benefit. The trial of Jesus was an awkward case for Pilate and learning that Jesus was from Galilee, he handed Him over to Herod Antipas, the tetrarch of Galilee (Luke 23:6-12). Pilate was not going to make a wrong move that would allow Herod Antipas to make another strike against him. Pilate was anxious to appease. He had nothing to lose and everything to gain. It worked! Herod Antipas returned Jesus to Pilate and they became friends on that day (Luke 23:12). Luke's statement gives the idea that at the trial they became friends and remained so from that time onward and so the A.D. 33 crucifixion date justifies Luke's statement as being accurate.

Here is another indication of the significance of the A.D. 33 date for Christ's death.

In conclusion, then, the A.D. 33 date is significant for New Testament interpretation in that it removes the charge that the Gospels are inaccurate and it fills several statements of the Gospel narratives with significant meaning.

SUMMARY AND CONCLUSION

The date of the crucifixion of Christ has been greatly debated. Scholars have dated it anywhere from A.D. 21 to 36.

To attempt to come to a concrete date, one must examine all the evidence at hand. First, it was seen that the officials at Christ's trial were Caiaphas and Pilate who were in office simultaneously from A.D. 26 to 36. This eliminates the A.D. 21 date. Next, in examining the day of crucifixion it was concluded that it occurred on Friday, Nisan 14. With the help of astronomy the only possible years on which Friday, Nisan 14 occurred were A.D. 27, 30, 33, and 36. One can eliminate A.D. 27 and 36 when one looks at the ministry of Christ, leaving only A.D. 30 and 33 as feasible dates. However, upon further examining the evidence of astronomy and the life of Christ the most viable date for the death of Christ was A.D. 33. This date is confirmed when one looks into history for it not only fills several passages of the Gospels with meaning but it also prevents the charge that the Gospels are inaccurate in some parts of the passion narrative.

Here, then, is the case for the A.D. 33 date for the crucifixion date of our Lord, more specifically Friday, April 3, A.D. 33.

Chapter VI

Daniel's Seventy Weeks and
New Testament Chronology

While Daniel was in the Babylonian captivity (605-538/ 37 B.C.), he was given the prophecy of the seventy weeks (Dan. 9:24-27), which has become the subject of many discussions and interpretations. The purpose of this chapter is to determine how this prophecy relates to the chronology of Christ's life discussed in the previous chapters in this book.

THE CONTEXT OF THE SEVENTY WEEKS

In the first year of Darius, 538/37 B.C. (Dan. 9:1; 2 Chron. 36:21-23; Ezra 1; 6:3-5), Daniel observed that the seventy-year captivity prophesied by Jeremiah (Jer. 25:11-12; 29:10) was nearing its completion. The reason for Israel's captivity was their refusal to obey the Word of the Lord from the prophets (Jer. 29:17-19) and to give their land sabbatical rests (2 Chron. 36:21). God had stated that Israel, because of her disobedience, would be removed from her land and scattered among the Gentiles until the land had enjoyed its sabbaths (Lev. 26:33-35).

According to 2 Chronicles 36:21 the land would be desolate for seventy years. One may therefore conclude that in the eight hundred year's history of Israel in the land, seventy sabbatical years were not kept. Now Daniel, seeing that the seventy years of captivity were nearing their completion, realized that before the exiles could return to their homeland they needed to confess and repent of their sin of disobedience before God (Lev. 26:40-46). Hence, Daniel confessed on behalf of his people the disobedient course they had followed and pleaded that God's anger would be turned away so that Israel might return to her land. While Daniel was making his petition, the angel Gabriel came to give him understanding of the prophetic message of the seventy weeks. Daniel had asked about Israel's imminent return to their land, but instead God gave him the revelation of the seventy weeks which was to assure Daniel that God would fulfill His covenant promises to the nation. Gabriel informed Daniel that God would bring Israel back into their land and set up the messianic kingdom. However, Gabriel went on to say that this would not be ultimately fulfilled at the end of the seventy-year captivity in Babylon but at the end of the seventy-week period stated in 9:24-27.

THE TERMINOLOGY OF THE SEVENTY WEEKS

INTRODUCTION

Over the centuries the meaning of the seventy weeks has been a *crux interpretum*. Some writers see the seventy weeks already fulfilled in some way during the Maccabean times.[1] Others view the weeks as merely symbolic. According to Young, "Since these numbers represent periods of time, the length of which is not stated, and since they are thus symbolical, it is not warrantable to seek to discover the precise lengths of the sevens."[2]

However, in the light of Daniel's inquiry about the consummation of a literal seventy-year captivity in Babylon, it seems most reasonable that the seventy weeks are not symbolical but must be interpreted literally. And as Wood observes, the fact of Daniel's use of definite numbers—seven, sixty-two, and one—makes it difficult to think of symbolical indefinite periods of time.[3] Hence in the light of the context the literal interpretation makes the most sense.

[1]James A. Montgomery, *A Critical and Exegetical Commentary on the Book of Daniel* (New York, 1927), pp. 390-401; George A. F. Knight, "The Book of Daniel," *The Interpreter's One-Volume Commentary on the Bible,* ed. by Charles M. Laymon (Nashville, 1971), pp. 447-48.
[2]Edward J. Young, *The Messianic Prophecies of Daniel* (Grand Rapids, 1954), p. 56; cf. H. C. Leupold, *Exposition of Daniel* (Columbus, OH, 1949), pp. 409-10; and C. F. Keil, *Biblical Commentary on the Book of Daniel,* trans. by M. G. Easton (Edinburgh, 1876), pp. 399-402.
[3]Leon Wood, *A Commentary on Daniel* (Grand Rapids, 1973), p. 247.

INTERPRETATION

The term שבעים in the Old Testament. The term שבעים is the plural form of שבוע which is a unit or period of seven, heptad, or week.[4] It is used twenty times in the Old Testament. Three times it means a unit of seven and is followed by ימים "days" (Ezek. 45:21; Dan. 10:2, 3); six times it means "week(s)," a normal seven-day week (Gen. 29:27, 28; Lev. 12:5; Deut. 16:9 *bis*; Jer. 5:24); five times it refers to the Feast of Weeks (Exod. 34:22; Num. 28:26; Deut. 16:10, 16; 2 Chron. 8:13); and six times it is used as a "unit of seven" without reference to days (Dan. 9:24, 25 *bis*, 26, 27*bis*). Therefore, the context determines its meaning. This can also be illustrated by עשׂור, which is normally translated "ten days" because the context demands this rendering thirteen out of sixteen occurrences in the Old Testament. However, three times (Ps. 33:2; 92:43; 144:9) it has reference to a musical instrument and would have to be translated "ten strings."[5] Thus עשׂור, has the idea of a "unit of ten" as determined by the context.

In conclusion the term שבוע means "a unit of seven" and its particular meaning must be determined by the particular context.

The term שבעים in Daniel 9:24-27. In this passage the term refers to units of seven years and thus Daniel is speaking of seventy of these units of seven years or a total of 490 years. The reasons for this conclusion are as follows:

First, in the context Daniel had been thinking in terms of years as well as multiples (ten times seven) of years (Dan. 9:1-2).

Second, Daniel had been considering Jeremiah 25:11 and 29:10 regarding the seventy-year captivity. The captivity was a result of violating the sabbatical year, which was to

[4]Francis Brown, S. R. Driver, and Charles Briggs (eds.), *A Hebrew and English Lexicon of the Old Testament* (Oxford, 1907), pp. 988-89; Ludwig Koehler and Walter Baumgartner (eds.), *Lexicon in Veteris Testamenti Libros* (Leiden, 1958), p. 940.
[5]Brown, Driver, and Briggs, p. 797.

have been observed after every six years (2 Chron. 36:21; cf. Lev. 26:34-35, 43). Each year of captivity represented one seven-year cycle in which the seventh or Sabbath year had not been observed. Thus it is clear that the context refers to years, not days. The seventy-year captivity was due to the Jews having violated seventy sabbatical years over a 490-year period and Daniel now saw seventy units of sevens decreed for another 490 years into Israel's future. This can be diagramed in the following way:

UNITS OF SEVENTY

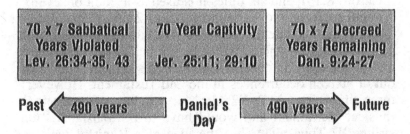

| 70 x 7 Sabbatical Years Violated Lev. 26:34-35, 43 | 70 Year Captivity Jer. 25:11; 29:10 | 70 x 7 Decreed Years Remaining Dan. 9:24-27 |

Past ← 490 years | Daniel's Day | 490 years → Future

Third, the only other usage of שבעים by Daniel is in 10:2, 3 where the phrase שלשה שבעים ימים is literally "three units of seven days" or twenty-one days. This has reference to Daniel's mourning for three weeks since the word ימים is included. The very fact that Daniel adds ימים indicates that he did not want his readers to think of the unit of seven the same way it was used in chapter nine. Everyone would have realized that Daniel would not have fasted twenty-one years, but the fact that he inserted ימים "days" in 10:2, 3 when it was not necessary would seem to indicate that he *would* have used ימים in 9:24-27 if there he meant 490 "days." Therefore, in 9:24-27 Daniel was referring to years and not days.

Fourth, it is impossible to fit the events described in 9:24-27, regardless of the *terminus a quo*, into 490 days or weeks. Only that number of years is viable.

Fifth, in 9:27 the covenant that will be confirmed for one "unit of seven" (שבוע) will be broken in the middle of that unit of seven. If one accepts the שָׁבוּעַ as a unit of seven years, this would mean that the covenant will be broken at the three and one-half year point and the last three and one-half years will be a time of trouble and desolation. This fits well with the trouble described by the temporal note "time, times, and half a time" in Daniel 7:25 and 12:7 as well as in Revelation 12:14.

Sixth, although the term שָׁבוּעַ does not refer to years elsewhere in the Bible it has this meaning in the Mishnah.[6]

In conclusion the term שבעים in Daniel 9 most reasonably refers to a unit of seven years. To make it anything else does not make good sense. However, for the sake of clarity this unit of seven years will be called "week(s)" for the remainder of this chapter, for it is simpler to refer to seventy "weeks" than to seventy "units of seven years." Therefore, Daniel's reference to seventy weeks means a period of 490 years.

THE TERMINUS A QUO OF THE SEVENTY WEEKS

Daniel 9:25 states that the starting point of the seventy weeks is the issuance of a command to restore and rebuild Jerusalem where a plaza (or square) and a moat (or trench) will be built during distressing times.

THE DESCRIPTION OF THE REBUILDING

Three things are to be noted in the description of the rebuilding of Jerusalem. First, the words לְהָשִׁיב וְלִבְנוֹת ("to restore and to rebuild") suggest that the city was raised to its former state. It is not a partial rebuilding but a complete restoration.[7]

Second, the words רְחוֹב וְחָרוּץ ("plaza and moat") give weight to the position for a complete restoration of the city. The first of these words means a plaza, street, or square,

---

[6]Mishnah: Baba Metzia ix. 10; Sanhedrin v. 1.
[7]For a fuller discussion of these terms, see E. W. Hengstenberg, *Christology of the Old Testament*, trans. by James Martin (2nd ed.; Edinburgh, 1872-78), III, 115-17.

"the broad spaces, generally just inside the city gates, the centre of city life."[8] It is a wide and free unoccupied place in the city (cf. Ezra 10:9; Esther 4:6; 2 Chron. 32:6; Neh. 8:1, 3). The second word, חרוץ, is more difficult to define. It is a passive participle of חרץ meaning "to cut, to sharpen, to decide."[9] In the Old Testament it is used fourteen times: four times it refers to a sharpened threshing instrument, a threshing sledge (Isa. 28:27; 41:15; Amos 1:3);[10] one time it suggests the idea of being maimed, cut, or mutilated (Lev. 22:22); six times it is used poetically of gold from the idea of the sharp bright color or from the idea that it is eagerly desired by men (חרץ can have the idea "to be eager, to covet") (Ps. 68:14 [13]; Prov. 3:14; 8:10, 19; 16:16; Zech. 9:3); two times it refers to "something decided," a strict decision as in the phrase "valley of decision" (Joel 3:14 *bis*); and once it is used in Daniel 9:25. Outside the Bible this term is used in Aramaic of a "trench;"[11] in Akkadian it has the idea of a "city moat;"[12] in the Qumran writings it is used of a "moat of the rampart or bulwark;"[13] and in mishnaic and targumic literature it has the idea of an incision, furrow, or trench.[14] Thus its basic idea is to make an incision, or cut or dig a trench.

Commentators are divided on how to apply the two words, רחוב וחרוץ, to Daniel 9:25, but it is best to take the first word *plaza* as referring to the interior of the city and the second word *trench* as referring to a moat going around the outside of the city. Part of Jerusalem's natural defenses consisted of a great cutting in the rock along the northern

---

[8]Montgomery, p. 380.
[9]Brown, Driver, and Briggs, p. 358.
[10]Joseph Reider, "Etymological Studies in Biblical Hebrew," *Vetus Testamentum* II (April, 1952), 116-17.
[11]Montgomery, p. 380.
[12]*Ibid.*
[13]M. Baillet, J. T. Milik, et R. de Vaux, *Les "Petites Grottes" de Qumrân*, 2 vols., *Discoveries in the Judaean Desert of Jordan*, III (Oxford, 1962), 244.
[14]Marcus Jastrow (comp.), *A Dictionary of the Targumin, the Talmud Bibli Yerushalmi, and the Midrashic Literature* (London, 1903), I, 502; cf. p. 505.

wall, which is still visible, for the purpose of building a defense wall.[15] Montgomery states that these "two items present a graphic picture of the complete restoration."[16]

Third, it should be noted that the rebuilding of Jerusalem would be done in times of distress or oppression.

In conclusion, then, Daniel describes the rebuilding of Jerusalem as being a complete restoration during troublous times.

THE TIME OF THE REBUILDING

Having discussed the description of the rebuilding of Jerusalem, one needs to determine when this occurred.

The decree of Cyrus. The first decree is the one of Cyrus to rebuild the temple, probably given on October 29, 539 B.C.[17] (2 Chron. 36:22-23; Ezra 1:1-4; 6:3-5). This decree concerned the return of the captives and the rebuilding of the temple but not a complete restoration of the city. However, Keil,[18] Leupold,[19] and Young[20] feel this decree marks the starting point of the seventy weeks. Young states:

> This edict [of Cyrus], furthermore, was issued in fulfillment of the prophecy of Jer., and it speaks expressly of going to Jerusalem and building there the temple — the first and most important step in rebuilding of the city. In this connection also one should consider the prophecies of Isa. 44:28 in which Cyrus is described as "saying to Jerusalem, Thou shalt be built; and to the temple, Thy foundation shall be laid." Likewise Isa. 45:13 declares of Cyrus, "he shall build my city, and he shall let go my captives." Lastly, it should be noted that the book of Ezra pictures Jerusalem as an existing city (cf. Ezra 4:12, 9:9).

> It cannot be denied that this was the year in which the effects of the going forth of a word began to appear in history.

[15]Montgomery, p. 380; Judah J. Slotki, *Daniel, Ezra and Nehemiah* (London, 1951), p. 78.
[16]Montgomery, p. 380.
[17]John C. Whitcomb, Jr., *Darius the Mede* (Grand Rapids, 1959), pp. 70-71.
[18]Keil, pp. 355-56.
[19]Leupold, pp. 417-26.
[20]Edward J. Young, *The Prophecy of Daniel: A Commentary* (Grand Rapids, 1949), pp. 202-3.

Cyrus issued the decree which brought an end to the exile and again turned the Jews toward Jerusalem. It is not justifiable to distinguish too sharply between the building of the city and the building of the temple. Certainly, if the people had received permission to return to Jerusalem to rebuild the temple, there was also implied in this permission to build for themselves homes in which to dwell. There is no doubt whatever but that the people thus understood the decree (cf. Haggai 1:2-4). The edict of Cyrus mentions the temple specifically, because that was the religious center of the city, that which distinguished it as the holy city of the Jews. If, therefore, we are to discover in history the effects of the going forth of a Divine word we discover them first appearing during the first year of Cyrus the king, and this year is thus to be regarded as the *terminus a quo* of the 70 sevens.[21]

While at first sight this all seems quite convincing, there are several problems with this view. First, Cyrus' edict refers to the rebuilding of the temple and not to the city. Although it is granted there were inhabitants and a city was built in Cyrus' time as predicted by Isaiah, certainly it was not a city that could defend itself as described in Daniel 9:25. Young cites two Scripture verses from Ezra to substantiate his view. The first passage — Ezra 4:12 (see also vv. 13 and 16) — is not applicable for it is referring not to Cyrus' time but to Artaxerxes' reign (465/64-423 B.C.) as even Young argues vigorously in another work of his.[22] The second passage — Ezra 9:9 — also refers to Artaxerxes' reign and not Cyrus' reign. Also the word for "wall," גדר, is a fence used to surround a vineyard and not a military defensive wall.[23] It is never used in Nehemiah in relation to building a defensive wall. Most likely it is metaphorically speaking of security brought about by the protection of the Persian kings.[24] The only other references to the walls in Ezra are the walls of the

[21]*Ibid.*
[22]Edward J. Young, *An Introduction to the Old Testament* (rev. ed.; Grand Rapids, 1960), pp. 403-4.
[23]Brown, Driver, and Briggs speak of it as a wall of stones without mortar, p. 173.
[24]C. F. Keil, *The Books of Ezra, Nehemiah, and Esther,* trans. by Sophia Taylor (Edinburgh, 1873), pp. 120-21; Slotki, p. 167.

temple (Ezra 5:3, 8, 9). Therefore, neither of these Scripture passages is in the context of the decree of Cyrus, and neither of these passages has any reference to the building of a defensive wall.

Second, a distinction should be made between the rebuilding of a city and the restoration of a city to its former state. Japan rebuilt itself after World War II, but that is quite different from restoring it to its pre-World War II military state. The commencement of the rebuilding began with Cyrus' decree but the city's complete restoration was not at that time.

Third, if one accepts the seventy weeks as beginning with Cyrus' decree, how does one reckon the 490 years? Young states:

> The 7 sevens apparently has [*sic*] reference to the time which should elapse between the issuance of the word and the completion of the city and temple; roughly, to the end of the period of Ezra and Neh. The 62 sevens follows [*sic*] this period. In vs. 25 these 62 sevens are not characterized, but in vs. 26 we are told what will happen after the expiry of the 62 sevens. The 62 sevens therefore have reference to the period which follows the age of Ezra and Neh. to the time of Christ.[25]

Though Young is not specific regarding the final week, it seems that he would make the first half of that week include all of Christ's incarnation and the destruction of the temple in A.D. 70, but with no indication of the *terminus ad quem* of the seventieth week.[26]

Young's formulation, according to the first seven weeks, would cover a period of about one hundred years (each week thus representing about fourteen years); the second period of sixty-two weeks would cover from Nehemiah to the time of Christ, a period of about 450 years

---

[25]Young, *Daniel,* pp. 205-6, 220; cf. Young, *Messianic Prophecies,* pp. 67-70.
[26]Young, *Daniel,* pp. 213-21; Young, *Messianic Prophecies,* pp. 69-84.

(each week representing about seven years); and the final week would be divided into two parts, the first half covering the life of Christ and going even until the destruction of the temple in A.D. 70, a period of thirty-five to seventy years (about ten to twenty years for each week), and the second half of the seventieth week would have no *terminus ad quem*. Of course, other scholars who begin the decree with Cyrus do not all calculate the seventieth week as Young does. However, it seems that this system makes havoc of Gabriel's sayings, which were rather specific. Also Young's lengthy explanation leads one to be suspicious of this interpretation. It seems highly subjective as is evident when one reads the various commentators who hold to a symbolical interpretation.

In conclusion, then, it is most *unlikely* that Cyrus' decree marks the *terminus a quo* of the seventy weeks described in Daniel.

The decree of Darius. The next decree in the restoration of the temple in Jerusalem was due to Tattenai, governor of Judah, who questioned the Jews' right to rebuild the temple (Ezra 5:3-17). Darius had a search made of Cyrus' decree and then issued a decree himself about 519/18 B.C. to confirm Cyrus' original decree (Ezra 6:1-12). This decree will not serve as the beginning date for the seventy weeks because it has specific reference to the temple and not to the city, and because it really is not a new decree but only confirms a former one.

The decree of Artaxerxes to Ezra. The third decree was the decree to Ezra in 457 B.C. It encouraged the return of more exiles with Ezra, the further enhancement of the temple and its accompanying worship, and the appointment of civil leaders (Ezra 7:11-26). Pusey,[27] Boutflower,[28] Payne,[29]

[27]E. B. Pusey, *Daniel the Prophet* (Oxford, 1876), pp. 164-233, esp. pp. 168-78.
[28]Charles Boutflower, *In and Around the Book of Daniel* (London, 1923), pp. 168-211.
[29]J. Barton Payne, *The Theology of the Older Testament* (Grand Rapids, 1962), pp. 276-78; J. Barton Payne, *The Imminent Appearing of Christ* (Grand Rapids, 1962), pp. 148-50; J. Barton Payne, *Encyclopedia of Biblical Prophecy* (New York, 1973), pp. 383-89.

and Goss[30] maintain that this decree to Ezra marked the *terminus a quo* of the seventy weeks and that the end of the sixty-ninth week brings one to A.D. 26 or 27 (depending on whether or not one dates the decree 458 or 457 B.C.), which marks the commencement of Christ's ministry. The proponents of this view (with the exception of Goss) would see at the middle of the seventieth week the crucifixion of Christ in A.D. 30 and the most likely *terminus ad quem* of the seventieth week would be in A.D. 33, the probable date of Stephen's death and Paul's conversion.

There are several problems with this view. First, and foremost, is that this decree has not a word about the rebuilding of the city of Jerusalem but rather the temple in Jerusalem.[31] This is even admitted by Payne.[32] The proponents of this theory say that a wall was permitted to be built because Artaxerxes gave unlimited freedom to use the leftover silver and gold (Ezra 7:18) and because Ezra was to appoint civil authorities (Ezra 7:25) who would want to build a wall. But the leftover silver and gold was to be used for the temple worship and the civil authorities were appointed for the purpose of judging and not for building defense walls.[33]

Second, to have the sixty-nine weeks terminate at the commencement of Christ's ministry in A.D. 26 or 27 is untenable for two reasons: (1) The cutting off of the Messiah (Dan. 9:26) is a very inappropriate way to refer to the descent of the Holy Spirit upon Jesus at the commencement of His ministry. (2) The date for the beginning of Jesus' ministry is not A.D. 26 or 27 but A.D. 29, as discussed previously.[34]

---

[30]Glenn Richard Goss, "The Chronological Problems of the Seventy Weeks of Daniel" (unpublished Th.D. dissertation, Dallas Theological Seminary, 1966), pp. 122-30.

[31]Keil, *Daniel,* p. 379; cf. Michael J. Gruenthaner, "The Seventy Weeks," *Catholic Biblical Quarterly,* I (January, 1939), 51.

[32]Payne, *Imminent Appearing,* p. 148.

[33]For a fuller discussion, see Fred Holtzman,"A Re-examination of the Seventy Weeks of Daniel" (unpublished Th.M. thesis, Dallas Theological Seminary, 1974), pp. 82-84.

[34]See Chapter II.

Third, to what does Daniel refer in 9:27 when he states he is confirming a covenant? If it refers to Christ, then what covenant was it and how did He break it?

Fourth, to say that the middle of the seventieth week refers to Christ's crucifixion in A.D. 30 is untenable on two grounds: (1) the sacrifices did not cease at Christ's crucifixion, and (2) though the date of A.D. 30 is possible the A.D. 33 date is far more plausible.[35]

Fifth, to say that the end of the seventieth week refers to Stephen's death and Paul's conversion in A.D. 33 is pure speculation. There is no hint of this in the texts of Daniel 9:27 and Acts 8-9 to denote the fulfillment of the seventieth week. Also, the dates of Paul's conversion as well as Stephen's martyrdom were more likely in A.D. 35.[36]

In conclusion, the decree of Artaxerxes to Ezra in 457 B.C. serving as the starting point of the seventy weeks is highly unlikely.

The decree of Artaxerxes to Nehemiah. The final decree is that of Artaxerxes to Nehemiah in 444 B.C. to rebuild the city of Jerusalem (Neh. 2:1-8). Several factors commend this decree as the one prophesied by Daniel (9:25) for the commencement of the seventy weeks. First, there is a direct reference to the restoration of the city (2:3, 5) and of the city gates and walls (2:3, 8). Second, Artaxerxes wrote a letter to Asaph to give materials to be used specifically for the walls (2:8). Third, the Book of Nehemiah and Ezra 4:7-23 indicate that certainly the restoration of the walls was done in the most distressing circumstances, as predicted by Daniel (Dan. 9:25). Fourth, no later decrees were given by the Persian kings pertaining to the rebuilding of Jerusalem.[37]

Keil objects to calling this a decree. He thinks it would more appropriately be seen as a "royal favor."[38] However,

---

[35]See Chapter V.
[36]Harold Hoehner, "Chronology of the Apostolic Age" (unpublished Th.D. dissertation, Dallas Theological Seminary, 1965), pp. 200-204; George Ogg, *The Odyssey of Paul* (Old Tappan, NJ, 1968), pp. 24-30.
[37]Cf. Albert Barnes, *Notes, Critical, Illustrative, and Practical, on the Book of Daniel* (New York, 1881), p. 390.
[38]Keil, *Daniel,* pp. 379-80.

Daniel 9:25, though not requiring a decree,[39] does require a command (דבר) and certainly this was the case with Artaxerxes as seen in the letters he wrote to the governors of the provinces beyond the river and to Asaph (Neh. 2:7-9).

In conclusion, this is the only decree that adequately fits the strictures given in Daniel 9:25. Hence this decree of Artaxerxes is considered the *terminus a quo* of the seventy weeks.

The date of this decree is given in the biblical record. Nehemiah 1:1 states that Nehemiah heard of Jerusalem's desolate conditions in the month of Chislev (November/December) in Artaxerxes' twentieth year. Then later in Artaxerxes' twentieth year in the month of Nisan (March/April) Nehemiah reports that he was granted permission to restore the city and build its walls (2:1). To have Nisan later than Chislev (in the same year) may seem strange until one realizes that Nehemiah was using a Tishri-to-Tishri (September/October) dating method rather than the Persian Nisan-to-Nisan method. Nehemiah was following what was used by the kings of Judah earlier in their history.[40] This method used by Nehemiah is confirmed by the Jews in Elephantine who also used this method during the same time period as Nehemiah.[41]

Next, one needs to establish the beginning of Artaxerxes' rule. His father Xerxes died shortly after December 17, 465 B.C.[42] and Artaxerxes immediately succeeded him. Since the accession-year system was used[43] the first year of Artaxerxes' reign according to the Persian Nisan-to-Nisan reckoning would be Nisan 464 to Nisan 463 and according to the Jewish Tishri-to-Tishri reckoning would be Tishri 464 to Tishri 463. This could be charted as shown at the top of page 128. Then the twentieth year of

[39]Goss, p. 120.
[40]Edwin R. Thiele, *The Mysterious Numbers of the Hebrew Kings* (rev. ed.; Grand Rapids, 1965), pp. 28-30, 161.
[41]S. H. Horn and L. H. Wood, "The Fifth-Century Jewish Calendar at Elephantine," *Journal of Near Eastern Studies*, XIII (January,1954), 4, 20.
[42]*Ibid.*, XIII, 9.
[43]*Ibid.*, XIII, 4.

THE ACCESSION OF ARTAXERXES

JULIAN (January New Year)	465		464		463	
PERSIAN (Nisan New Year)	21st Year of Xerxes	Accession Year of Artaxerxes	1st Year of Artaxerxes' Reign		2nd Year	▶
JEWISH (Tishri New Year)		21st Year of Xerxes	Accession Year of Artaxerxes	1st Year of Artaxerxes' Reign	2nd Year	▶

XERXES' DEATH, ARTAXERXES' ACCESSION, DECEMBER 465

Artaxerxes' reign, mentioned in Nehemiah 1:1 and 2:1, would be charted as shown at the top of page 129.

In conclusion, the report to Nehemiah (1:1) occurred in Chislev (November/December) of 445 B.C. and the decree of Artaxerxes (2:1) occurred in Nisan (March/April) of 444 B.C.[44]

Therefore, Nisan 444 B.C. marks the *terminus a quo* of the seventy weeks of Daniel 9:24-27.

THE TERMINUS AD QUEM OF THE SIXTY-NINE WEEKS

THE CUMULATION OF THE SEVEN WEEKS AND THE SIXTY-TWO WEEKS

In Daniel 9:25 does the clause "the going forth of the decree to restore and rebuild Jerusalem until Messiah the

[44]Richard A. Parker and Waldo H. Dubberstein, *Babylonian Chronology 626 B.C.—A.D. 75* (2nd ed.; Providence, 1956), p. 32; Herman H. Goldstine, *New and Full Moons, 1001 B.C. to A.D. 1651* (Philadelphia, 1973), p. 47.

THE DECREE OF ARTAXERXES

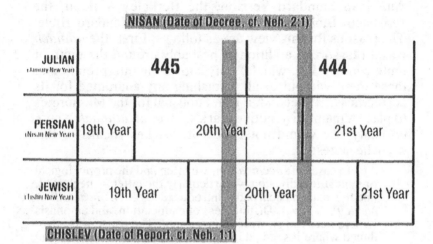

	NISAN (Date of Decree, cf. Neh. 2:1)				
JULIAN (January New Year)	**445**			**444**	
PERSIAN (Nisan New Year)	19th Year		20th Year	21st Year	
JEWISH (Tishri New Year)	19th Year		20th Year		21st Year
	CHISLEV (Date of Report, cf. Neh. 1:1)				

Prince" refer only to the seven weeks or to the seven weeks and sixty-two weeks, making it a total of sixty-nine weeks? Because of the *athnach* (a major disjunctive punctuation mark) under the "seven weeks" in the Massoretic text it is thought by some commentators[45] that there should be a major break after these words and thus the words "sixty-two weeks" begin a new sentence. This rendering is seen in the Revised Standard Version, the Confraternity Version, and the New English Bible.

However, most commentators[46] think that the seven weeks and the sixty-two weeks are successive or continuous making a total of sixty-nine weeks between the decree to

---

[45]E.g., Montgomery, pp. 378-80; Leupold, pp. 417-24.
[46]E.g., Keil, *Daniel*, pp. 350-58; Hengstenberg, III, 122-25; Boutflower, pp. 190-91; Young, *Daniel*, p. 205; Norman W. Porteous, *Daniel: A Commentary* (London, 1965), p. 141; Knight, p. 448; Wood, pp. 252-54.

restore Jerusalem and Messiah the Prince. This is followed in the Septuagint (in v. 27), Theodotion, Syriac, and Vulgate versions as well as the Authorized Version, Douay Version, American Standard Version, the Berkeley Version, the Jerusalem Bible, and the New American Standard Bible. The reasons for this view are as follows: First, the *athnach* was a Massoretic addition of probably around the ninth or tenth century A.D. which "only shows the interpretation of these men, without at all furnishing any guarantee for its correctness."[47] Second, it is not unusual for the Massoretes to place a major disjunctive mark such as an *athnach* where normally one would not expect it. Wickes speaks of this when he states:

> In cases of *specification,* we often find the proper logical or syntactical division — particularly the latter — neglected, and the main musical pause introduced *between the details* or *particulars given*. Distinctness of enunciation, and emphasis (where necessary), were thus secured. The pause was introduced where it seemed likely to be most effective. Thus the *logical* division is disregarded: . . .
>
> . . . *Syntactical* clauses are treated in the same way, and subject, object, & c. are cut in two — or members that belong together, separated — by the dichotomy. (A logical pause may occur in the verse or not.)[48]

Wickes cites several examples of this phenomenon (Gen. 7:13; 25:20; Exod. 35:23; Lev. 16:2; Isa. 49:21; 66:19) but the most relevant passage he cites is Numbers 28:19: "And ye shall offer a burnt-offering unto Jehovah, two young bullocks and one ram,|[=an *athnach*] and seven he-lambs of the first year; they shall be unto you without blemish."[49] In this verse one sees no logical reason for the *athnach* there. Third, to place a break between the seven weeks and the sixty-two weeks is foreign to the context and makes no

---

[47]Keil, *Daniel,* p. 356.
[48]William Wickes, *A Treatise on the Accentuation of the Twenty-one So-called Prose Books of the Old Testament* (Oxford, 1887), pp. 40-41; reprint ed., *Two Treatises on the Accentuation of the Old Testament* II (New York, 1970), 40-41.
[49]*Ibid.,* II, 41.

sense.[50] This means that it took 434 years to build the plaza and moat, which does not fit historically nor what was intended by Daniel in the context.

In conclusion, then, the seven weeks and sixty-two weeks need to be considered cumulative or continuous and not parallel or contemporaneous. Thus it is a total of sixty-nine weeks from the going forth of the decree to restore and rebuild Jerusalem until the Messiah the Prince.

THE SEPARATION OF THE SIXTY-NINTH FROM THE SEVENTIETH WEEK

Keil, Leupold, Payne, Young, and others say that the seventieth week follows immediately after the sixty-ninth week. However, it is far more plausible to see the sixty-nine weeks fulfilled historically and the seventieth week as yet unfulfilled. The reasons are as follows: First, to view the six things in Daniel 9:24 — to finish the transgression, to make an end of sin, to make atonement for iniquity, to bring in everlasting righteousness, to seal up vision and prophecy, and to anoint the most holy place — as having been fulfilled in Christ's death at His first advent is impossible. All these have reference to the nation of Israel and none of these has been fulfilled to that nation. Israel has not yet finished her transgression, nor been purged of her iniquity. Nor has she experienced the everlasting righteousness promised her. Paul sees this still in the future for Israel (Rom. 11:25-27).[51] The anointing of the most holy is not a reference to Christ's anointing, as Young would have it;[52] instead the "most holy" (קֹדֶשׁ קָדָשִׁים) are technical words that are always translated in the Old Testament by the phrase the "holy of holies."

Second, the Messiah was cut off "after" the sixty-ninth week and not "during" the seventieth. Gundry stated it well when he wrote:

---

[50]Hengstenberg, III, 123; Young, *Daniel*, p. 205.
[51]Robert H. Gundry, *The Church and the Tribulation* (Grand Rapids, 1973), p. 189.
[52]Young, *Daniel*, p. 201.

If the cutting off of the Messiah occurred in the middle of the seventieth week, it is very strange that the cutting off is said to be "after" the sixty-nine weeks (figuring the sum of the seven and the sixty-two weeks). Much more naturally the text would have read "during" or "in the midst of" the seventieth week, as it does in verse twenty-seven concerning the stoppage of the sacrifices. The only adequate explanation for this unusual turn of expression is that the seventieth week did not follow on the heels of the sixty-ninth, but that an interval separates the two. The crucifixion then comes shortly "after" the sixty-ninth but not within the seventieth because of an intervening gap. The possibility of a gap between the sixty-ninth and the seventieth weeks is established by the well-accepted OT phenomenon of prophetic perspective, in which gaps such as that between the first and second advents were not perceived.[53]

An example of a gap between the two advents of Christ is seen in Luke 4:18-19 when Christ quoted Isaiah 61:1-2 leaving in the words referring to His first advent but omitting the words referring to His second advent.

Third, the person who confirms the covenant in Daniel 9:27 cannot refer to Christ.[54] (1) The nearest antecedent is "the prince who is to come," in verse 26.[55] (2) At no time in Christ's ministry did He confirm an already-existing covenant. Certainly Payne's attempt to say that Christ "cause[d] to prevail" an existing covenant rather than making a new covenant on the basis of the absence of the word "new" in some Greek manuscripts in Matthew 26:28[56] is tenuous to say the least, for, as Gundry points out, the adjective "new" is in Luke 22:20 and 1 Corinthians 11:25 and the new covenant is twice quoted in Hebrews.[57] (3) If Christ did confirm a covenant in His first advent, when did He break it? Would

[53]Gundry, p. 190.
[54]A recent attempt to bolster the idea that Christ is the one who makes the covenant is by Meredith G. Kline, "The Covenant of the Seventieth Week," *The Law and the Prophets. Old Testament Studies Prepared in Honor of Oswald Thompson Allis*, ed. by John H. Skilton (Nutley, NJ, 1974), pp. 452-69, esp. pp. 461-69.
[55]John F. Walvoord, *Daniel: The Key to Prophetic Revelation* (Chicago, 1971), p. 234.
[56]Payne, *Imminent Appearing*, p. 151.
[57]Gundry, pp. 190-91.

Christ break a covenant He has made? Thus the covenant-confirmer does not refer to Christ but to a prince who is yet to come.

Fourth, Christ's death did render inoperative the animal sacrifices but did *not* cause them to cease immediately. In fact, the Jews sacrificed animals until Jerusalem's destruction in A.D. 70.

Fifth, the abomination of desolation has not yet been fulfilled. In Matthew 24:15 Jesus said that it would occur after His ministry on earth. He spoke of the appearance of the abomination of desolation in the Jerusalem temple as a signal of the great tribulation which is immediately followed by Christ's second advent. It is true that Jerusalem suffered destruction in A.D. 66-70 but Christ did not return in A.D. 70. In fact, the Book of Revelation speaks of Jerusalem's desolation as yet future and not as having been fulfilled nearly a quarter century before its composition.[58]

Sixth, the person in view in Daniel 9:27 correlates very well with the wicked person in 7:25 and in Revelation 12 and 13, who has not yet appeared and been judged as described in Revelation 19.

Seventh, the events of the last half of the seventieth week, described in Daniel 9:27b, fit well into the second three and one-half years of the tribulation described in the Book of Revelation, which is yet future.

In conclusion, it is far better to see an intervening gap between the sixty-ninth and seventieth weeks than to view the seventieth as following the sixty-ninth. The seventieth week is yet to be fulfilled. The sixty-nine weeks have been fulfilled and there now needs to be a discussion as to how it relates chronologically to Christ's ministry on earth.

THE COMPLETION OF THE SIXTY-NINE WEEKS

Thus far it has been concluded that the *terminus a quo* of the seventy weeks is Nisan 444 B.C. After the sixty-two weeks the Messiah will be cut off and have nothing (Dan.

---

[58]*Ibid.,* p. 191.

9:26).[59] This has reference to Christ's death and indicates that in His first advent He would not acquire the messianic kingdom envisioned in the Old Testament. Thus the sixty-nine weeks were to expire shortly before Christ's death. Hence the *terminus ad quem* for the sixty-ninth week is shortly before Christ's death. In the previous chapters in this book this writer concluded that Christ's death occurred on Friday, Nisan 14 in A.D. 33 (Friday, April 3, A.D. 33, on the Julian calendar).

Calculation with the solar year. If one multiplies the sixty-nine weeks by seven solar years, the total is 483 years. Subtracting this from 444 B.C. gives the date of A.D. 38, five years after Christ's crucifixion. So it is obvious that a calculation using the solar year does not work.

Calculation with the sabbatical year. A new attempt has been made by Newman who calculates sixty-nine sabbatical years between the *termini a quo* and *ad quem* of the sixty-nine weeks. His conclusion is that the sixty-ninth sabbatical year was A.D. 27-34.[60] However, there are some problems with this view. To begin with, the first sabbatical period would be from 452 to 445 B.C., which is one year before the decree of Artaxerxes to Nehemiah. Thus one would have only sixty-eight sabbatical years between the decree and Christ's death. Second, Daniel says that the Messiah would be cut off after the sixty-nine weeks, and thus according to Newman's view Christ would have to be cut off after A.D. 34, a year after His crucifixion. Third, the figures in Daniel seem to be more specific than sabbatical years. If sabbatical years were used, one would expect the decree to have been given in a sabbatical year and Christ's death to have occurred in a sabbatical year. Fourth, although the seventy-year captivity was for Israel's disobedience in not observing the sabbatical

---

[59]C. G. Ozanne, "Three Textual Problems in Daniel," *The Journal of Theological Studies,* XVI (October, 1965), 446-47.
[60]Robert C. Newman, "Daniel's Seventy Weeks and the Old Testament Sabbath-Year Cycle," *Journal of the Evangelical Theological Society,* XVI (Fall, 1973), 232-34.

years, there is no specific reference to sabbatical years mentioned in the immediate context. Fifth, there is no direct biblical evidence as to which year the sabbatical year occurred. All the evidence Newman gives is from secondary sources. Therefore, this system of calculation does not solve the problem.

Calculation with the 360-day year. The solution that is the most plausible is the one introduced by Anderson. He proposed that the length of the year should be calculated as 360 days. He called these 360-day years "prophetic years."[61]

This makes good sense for several reasons. First, with modern astronomy one can reckon a year very precisely as being "365.24219879 days, or 365 days, 5 hours, 48 minutes, 45.975 seconds."[62] However, in ancient times various systems were used. When one investigates the calendars of ancient India,[63] Persia,[64] Babylonia and Assyria,[65] Egypt,[66]

[61]Robert Anderson, *The Coming Prince* (5th ed.; London, 1895), pp. 67-75.
[62]Jack Finegan, *Handbook of Biblical Chronology* (Princeton, 1964), p. 19.
[63]For the calendars of various countries, Velikovsky gives extensive documentation. Immanuel Velikovsky, *Worlds in Collision* (Garden City, NY, 1950), pp. 330-32; Jean Lucien Antoine Filiozat, "Calendar, V. Hindu Calendar," *Encyclopaedia Britannica*, IV (14th ed., 1972), 621; J. A. B. van Buitenen, "Calendar, IV. The Far East: The Hindu Calendar," *Encyclopaedia Britannica*, III (15th ed., 1974), 607.
[64]Velikovsky, pp. 332-33; E. J. Bickerman, "Calendar, III. Ancient Middle Eastern Calendar Systems: Lunisolar Calendars in Antiquity," *Encyclopaedia Britannica*, III (15th ed., 1974), 605.
[65]Velikovsky, pp. 333-35; Hildegard Lewy, "Calendar, VI. Babylonian and Assyrian Calendars," *Encyclopaedia Britannica*, IV (14th ed., 1972), 623; Bickerman, *Encyclopaedia Britannica*, III, 604; cf. Horn and Wood, *Journal of Near Eastern Studies*, XIII, 5.
[66]Velikovsky, pp. 123-24, 336-38; T. Eric Poet, "Calendar, IV. Egyptian Calendar," *Encyclopaedia Britannica*, VI (14th ed., 1972), 620-21; Margaret Stefana Drower, "Chronology, III. Egyptian," *Encyclopaedia Britannica*, V (14th ed., 1972), 723; John D. Schmidt, "Calendar, III. Ancient Middle Eastern Calendar Systems: The Egyptian Calendar," *Encyclopaedia Britannica*, III (15th ed., 1974), 606; Wolfgang Helck, "Chronology: Egyptian," *Encyclopaedia Britannica*, IV (15th ed., 1974), 575; Finegan, pp. 29, 32; Horn and Wood, *Journal of Near Eastern Studies*, XIII, 3.

Central and South America,[67] and China[68] it is interesting to notice that they uniformly had twelve thirty-day months (a few had eighteen twenty-day months) making a total of 360 days for the year and they had various methods of intercalating days so that the year would come out correctly. Although it may be strange to present-day thinking, it was common in those days to think of a 360-day year.

Second, in conjunction with the prophetic literature of the Bible, the 360-day year is used. Daniel's seventieth week is a good illustration of this fact. A covenant will be confirmed for the seven years of the seventieth week (Dan. 9:27) but it will be broken in the middle of the week. In the last half of the week, or for three and one-half years, there will be the terrible persecution. This matches with the persecution mentioned in 7:24-25, which will last for "a time, times, and half a time," or three and one-half years. This phrase is also mentioned in 12:7. However, it is not until one comes to the New Testament that the duration of the year is known. John uses the same terminology of time, times, and half a time in Revelation 12:14. Speaking of the same situation within the same chapter, John says that the persecution will be for 1,260 days (12:6). John again uses this figure of 1,260 days in 11:3 and that period is also listed as being forty-two months in the previous verse (11:2). Also, the forty-two month period is mentioned in 13:5, which speaks of the same period of persecution. Thus the forty-two months equals the 1,260 days, and that equals the time, times, and half a time or three and one-half years, which in turn equals the half week in Daniel 9:27. Hence the month is thirty days and the year is 360 days.

Third, outside the prophetic literature the 360-day year is used one other time in the Bible. Genesis 7:11 states that the flood began on the seventeenth day of the second month. According to Genesis 8:4 the flood ended on the seventeenth

[67]Velikovsky, pp. 339-40; Tatiana Proskouriakoff, "Calendar, V. Calendar Systems of the Americas," *Encyclopaedia Britannica*, III (15th ed., 1974), 609-11; J. Eric S. Thompson, "Chronology: Pre-Columbian American," *Encyclopaedia Britannica*, IV (15th ed., 1974), 581.
[68]Velikovsky, p. 340.

day of the seventh month, exactly five months later. Genesis 7:24 and 8:3 state that the duration of the flood was 150 days. Hence five months equals 150 days or each month equals thirty days.

Therefore, in the light of these observations the 360-day year should not be too surprising.

Does the 360-day year correlate with the date of the cutting off of the Messiah? Anderson multiplies the sixty-nine weeks by seven years for each week by 360 days and comes to the total of 173,880 days. His *terminus a quo* for the sixty-nine weeks is Nisan 1 in Artaxerxes' twentieth year or March 14, 445 B.C., and his *terminus ad quem* is the triumphal entry on Nisan 10, April 6, A.D. 32. He shows that this works out perfectly. The time between 445 B.C. and A.D. 32 is 476 years; multiplying 476 by 365 days totals 173,740 days. He adds 116 days for leap years and 24 days for the difference between March 14 (of 445 B.C.) and April 6 (of A.D. 32) and thus arrives at a total of 173,880 days.[69]

Anderson's calculations include some problems. First, in the light of new evidence since Anderson's day, the 445 B.C. date is not acceptable for Artaxerxes' twentieth year; instead the decree was given in Nisan, 444 B.C. Second, the A.D. 32 date for the crucifixion is untenable. It would mean that Christ was crucified on either a Sunday or Monday.[70] In fact, Anderson realizes the dilemma and he has to do mathematical gymnastics to arrive at a Friday crucifixion. This makes one immediately suspect. Actually there is no good evidence for an A.D. 32 crucifixion date.

In previous chapters in this book it was concluded that Christ's crucifixion occurred on Friday, Nisan 14, in A.D. 33. Reckoning His death according to the Julian calendar, Christ died on Friday, April 3, A.D. 33.[71] As discussed

[69]Anderson, pp. 119-29.
[70]J. K. Fotheringham, "The Evidence of Astronomy and Technical Chronology for the Date of the Crucifixion," *The Journal of Theological Studies,* XXXV (April, 1934), 162.
[71]See Goldstine, p. 87; Parker and Dubberstein, p. 46; Fotheringham, *The Journal of Theological Studies,* XXXV, 142-62; Joachim Jeremias, *The Eucharistic Words of Jesus,* trans. by Norman Perrin (3rd ed.; London, 1966), p. 38.

above, the *terminus a quo* occurred in Nisan, 444 B.C. Although Nehemiah 2:1 does not specify which day of Nisan the decree to rebuild Jerusalem occurred, it cannot have occurred before Nisan 1. This study will assume Nisan 1[72] as the *terminus a quo* although realizing it could have occurred on some other day in Nisan. Nisan 1 in 444 B.C. was March 4, or more likely March 5 since the crescent of the new moon would have been first visible so late at night (*ca.* 10p.m.) on March 4 and could easily have been missed.[73]

Using the 360-day year the calculation would be as follows. Multiplying the sixty-nine weeks by seven years for each week by 360 days gives a total of 173,880 days. The difference between 444 B.C. and A.D. 33, then, is 476 solar years. By multiplying 476 by 365.24219879 or by 365 days, 5 hours, 48 minutes, 45.975 seconds, one comes to 173,855.28662404 days or 173,855 days, 6 hours, 52 minutes, 44 seconds. This leaves only 25 days to be accounted for between 444 B.C. and A.D. 33. By adding the 25 days to March 5 (of 444 B.C.), one comes to March 30 (of A.D. 33) which was Nisan 10 in A.D. 33. This is the triumphal entry of Jesus into Jerusalem.

SUMMARY AND CONCLUSION

Daniel inquired about the termination of the seventy-year captivity. Gabriel said that Israel would not come to its messianic rest until seventy weeks were completed. It was concluded that the seventy weeks refer to 490 years, which

---

[72]Anderson (p. 108) states: "The Persian edict which restored the autonomy of Judah was issued in the Jewish month of Nisan. It may in fact have been dated the 1st of Nisan, but no other day being named, the prophetic period must be reckoned, according to a practice common with the Jews, from the Jewish New Year's Day. The seventy weeks are therefore to be computed from the 1st of Nisan . . ." Anderson cites the mishnaic tractate *Rosh ha-Shanah* (i. 1) as evidence to support his thesis. His reasoning may be questioned at three points: (1) In his second sentence quoted above he is not sure of the date in the first half but is absolutely sure in the second half. (2) One would question the validity of assuming that what was true in the mishnaic era was true in Nehemiah's time. (3) The Jewish New Year was not Nisan 1 but Tishri 1.
[73]Goldstine, p. 47.

are to be calculated according to the prophetic year of 360 days. The *terminus a quo* of this seventy-week period was reckoned as being March 4 or 5 (more probably the latter). It was decided that there is a gap between the sixty-ninth and the seventieth week. The *terminus ad quem* of the sixty-ninth week was on the day of Christ's triumphal entry on March 30, A.D. 33.

As predicted in Zechariah 9:9, Christ presented Himself to Israel as Messiah the king for the last time and the multitude of the disciples shouted loudly by quoting from a messianic psalm: "Blessed is the king who comes in the name of the Lord" (Ps. 118:26; Matt. 21:9; Mark 11:10; Luke 19:38; John 12:13). This occurred on Monday, Nisan 10 (March 30) and only four days later on Friday, Nisan 14, April 3, A.D. 33, Jesus was cut off or crucified.

The seventieth week of Daniel's prophecy is yet to be fulfilled. When that is accomplished, Daniel's inquiry will be fully realized for Israel will be back in her homeland with her Messiah.

Daniel's Seventy Weeks

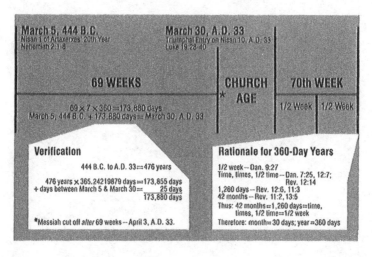

@1975 By Dallas Theological Seminary. This chart may not be reproduced in any form without prior written permission.

Chapter VII

Conclusion

Jesus Christ entered into the history of our world in the winter of 5/4 B.C. shortly before the death of Herod the Great. The only thing recorded of Jesus' youth is the time when He was twelve and had a discussion with the rabbis after the Passover (A.D. 9). Shortly after John the Baptist began his ministry Jesus began His in the summer or autumn of A.D. 29. His ministry was full—lasting three and a half years. Before His last Passover there was the triumphal entry on Monday, Nisan 10, March 30, A.D. 33. This marked the end of the sixty-nine weeks of Daniel 9:24-26. Later that week He was "cut off" with the betrayal, arrest, and trial which led to His crucifixion on Friday, April 3, 33.

Although it is not usual to write the conclusion in the first person singular, I think it may be of interest to some to know how I came to the conclusions presented in this book. Have I always held to the dates mentioned in this book? Not at all. It has been a long journey. It began in the mid-sixties while I was working on a doctoral dissertation on Herod Antipas at Cambridge University. Working on an appendix on the commencement of John the Baptist's ministry (Luke 3:1-2), I was convinced that John's ministry had to begin no later than September of A.D. 27. Having held to the A.D. 30 date for crucifixion, I attempted to keep that date and accept a two-year ministry. But this view has its own inherent problems as seen in chapter III. Thus the only other feasible date for the crucifixion is A.D. 33. Finally, in accepting this date all the pieces began to fit together scripturally, astronomically, and politically.

The conclusions of the final chapter were developed

over a period of time. The dating of Artaxerxes' accession was settled while I was teaching a course on the Minor Prophets, attempting to furnish a chronological background for them. Then later working with the day of crucifixion it seemed that a Monday triumphal entry of Christ best fit the evidence. Since I had already accepted the A.D. 33 date for the crucifixion, could all these things be reconciled with Daniel's prophecy of the seventy weeks? Not knowing what conclusions would result, I attempted to bring all the facets together and the final results were better than had been anticipated.

In conclusion, it is hoped that the discussion of this study will lead one to a greater appreciation of the life and ministry of Jesus Christ.

CHRONOLOGICAL TABLE OF CHRIST'S LIFE

Christ's birth	winter 5/4 B.C.
Herod the Great's death	March/April 4 B.C.
Prefects began to rule over Judea and Samaria	A.D. 6
Christ at the temple when twelve	Passover, April 29, 9
Caiaphas became high priest	A.D. 18
Pilate arrived in Judea	A.D. 26
Commencement of John the Baptist's ministry	A.D. 29
Commencement of Christ's ministry	summer/autumn A.D. 29
Christ's first Passover (John 2:13)	April 7, 30
John the Baptist imprisoned	A.D. 30 or 31
Christ's second Passover	April 25, 31
John the Baptist's death	A.D. 31 or 32
Christ at the Feast of Tabernacles (John 5:1)	October 21-28, 31
Christ's third Passover (John 6:4)	April 13/14, 32
Christ at the Feast of Tabernacles (John 7:2, 10)	September 10-17, 32
Christ at the Feast of Dedication (John 10:22-39)	December 18, 32
Christ's final week	March 28 — April 5, 33
Arrived at Bethany	Saturday, March 28
Crowds at Bethany	Sunday, March 29
Triumphal entry	Monday, March 30
Cursed the fig tree and cleansed temple	Tuesday, March 31
Temple controversy and Olivet discourse	Wednesday, April 1
Christ ate Passover, betrayed, arrested, and tried	Thursday, April 2
Christ tried and crucified	Friday, April 3
Christ laid in the tomb	Saturday, April 4
Christ resurrected	Sunday, April 5
Christ's ascension (Acts 1)	Thursday, May 14, 33
Day of Pentecost (Acts 2)	Sunday, May 24, 33

BIBLIOGRAPHY

Primary Sources

Appian. *Roman History*. 4 vols. with English translation by Horace White. Loeb Classical Library. London, 1912-13.

The Babylonian Talmud. 18 vols. Translated and edited by I. Epstein. London, 1961.

Baillet, M.; Milik, J.T.; and Vaux, R. de. *Les "Petites Grottes" de Qumrân*. 2 vols. *Discoveries in the Judaean Desert of Jordan*. 7 vols. Oxford, 1955-68.

Biblia Hebraica. Edited by Rud. Kittel. 3rd ed. Stuttgart, 1954.

Corpus Inscriptionum Graecarum. 4 vols. Edited by Augustus Boeckhius, *et al.* Berlin, 1828-77.

Corpus Iuris Civilis. 3 vols. Edited by Paul Krueger, Theodor Mommsen, and Rudolf Schoell. Berlin, 1872-95.

Dio Cassius. *Roman History*. 9 vols. with English translation by Earnest Cary. Loeb Classical Library. London, 1914-27.

Εὐαγγέλιον Κατὰ Πέτρον. *The Akhmîn Fragment of the Apocryphal Gospel of St Peter*. Edited with introduction, notes by Henry Barclay Swete. London, 1893.

Eusebius. *Chronica*. Edited by Rudolf Helm. Vol XXIV of *Die griechischen christlichen Schriftsteller*. Leipzig, 1913.

————. *The Ecclesiastical History*. 2 vols. with English translation by Kirsopp Lake and J. E. L. Oulton. Loeb Classical Library. London, 1926-32.

The Greek New Testament. Edited by Kurt Aland, *et al.* 3rd ed. Stuttgart, 1975.

Josephus. 9 vols. with English translation by H. St. Thackeray, Ralph Marcus, and Louis H. Feldman. Loeb Classical Library. London, 1926-65.

Midrash Rabbah. 10 vols. Translated and edited by H. Freedman and Maurice Simon. London, 1961.

The Mishnah. Translated by H. Danby. London, 1933.

Patrologia Graeca. 161 vols. Edited by J.-P. Migne. Paris, 1857-1936.

Patrologia Latina. 221 vols. Edited by J.-P. Migne. Paris, 1844-1963.

Philo. 10 vols. with English translation by F. H. Colson, G. H. Whitaker, and Ralph Marcus. Loeb Classical Library. London, 1929-53.

Philonis Alexandrini. *Legatio ad Gaium*. Edited with introduction, translation, and commentary by E. Mary Smallwood. Leiden, 1961.

Plutarch. *Lives*. 10 vols. with English translation by Bernadotte Perrin. Loeb Classical Library. London, 1914-26.

Septuagint. 2 vols. Edited by Alfred Rahlfs. 5th ed. Stuttgart, 1952.

Strabo. *The Geography of Strabo*. 8 vols. with English translation by Horace Leonard Jones. Loeb Classical Library. London, 1917-32.

Suetonius. *The Lives of the Caesars and the Lives of Illustrious Men*. 2 vols. with English translation by J. C. Rolfe. Loeb Classical Library. London, 1914.

Synopsis Quattuor Evangeliorum. Edited by Kurt Aland. 4th ed. Stuttgart, 1965.

Tacitus. *The Annals*. 3 vols. with English translation by John Jackson. Loeb Classical Library. London, 1931-37.

_____. *The Histories*. 2 vols. with English translation by Clifford H. Moore. Loeb Classical Library. London, 1925-31.

Le Talmud de Jérusalem. 12 vols. Translated by Moise Schwab. Paris, 1871-90.

Thucydides. *History of the Pelopennesian War*. 4 vols. with English translation by Charles Forster Smith. Loeb Classical Library. London, 1919-23.

Books

Anderson, Robert. *The Coming Prince*. 5th ed. London, 1895.

Andrews, Samuel J. *The Life of Our Lord upon the Earth*. 4th ed. New York, 1891.

Arndt, William F. *The Gospel according to St. Luke*. St. Louis, 1956.

Baly, Denis. *The Geography of the Bible*. New York, 1957.

Barnes, Albert. *Notes, Critical, Illustrative, and Practical, on the Book of Daniel*. New York, 1881.

Barrett, C. K. *The Gospel according to St. John*. London, 1956.

Bauer, Walter. *A Greek-English Lexicon of the New Testament and Other Early Christian Literature*. Translation and adaptation of the 4th revised and augmented edition by William F. Arndt and F. Wilbur Gingrich. Cambridge and Chicago, 1957.

Bellinger, A. R. *The Coins*. Final Report VI of *The Excavations at Dura-Europos*. Edited by M. I. Rostovtzeff, *et al*. New Haven, 1949.

Bengel, John Albert. *Gnomon of the New Testament*. 5 vols. Translated by Andrew R. Fausset, *et al*. 2nd ed. Edinburgh, 1859.

Bernard, J. H. *A Critical Commentary on the Gospel according to St. John*. Edited by A. H. McNeile. Edinburgh, 1928.

Bevan, E. *Holy Images*. London, 1940.

Blass, F. and Debrunner, A. *A Greek Grammar of the New Testament and Other Early Christian Literature*. Translated by Robert W. Funk. Chicago, 1961.

Blinzler, Josef. *The Trial of Jesus*. Translated by Isabel and Florence McHugh. 2nd ed. Westminster, MD, 1959.

Boa, Kenneth D. "The Star of Bethlehem." Unpublished Th.M. thesis, Dallas Theological Seminary, 1972.

Bornkamm, Günther. *Jesus of Nazareth*. Translated by Irene and Fraser McLuskey with James M. Robinson. London, 1960.

Boutflower, Charles. *In and Around the Book of Daniel*. London, 1923.

Brandon, S. F. G. *Jesus and the Zealots*. Manchester, 1967.

————. *The Trial of Jesus of Nazareth*. London, 1968.

Brown, Francis; Driver, S. R.; and Briggs, Charles, eds. *A Hebrew and English Lexicon of the Old Testament*. Oxford, 1907.

Brown, Raymond E. *The Gospel according to John*. 2 vols. Garden City, NY, 1966-70.

Bruce, F. F. *New Testament History*. London, 1969.

Bultmann, Rudolf. *The Gospel of John*. Translated by G. R. Beasley-Murray, R. W. N. Hoare, and J. K. Riches. Philadelphia, 1971.

Calvin, John. *The Gospel according to St. John*. 2 pts. Translated by T. H. L. Parker. Grand Rapids, 1959-60.

Caspari, C. E. *A Chronological and Geographical Introduction to the Life of Christ*. Translated by Maurice J. Evans. Edinburgh, 1876.

Cheney, Johnston M. *The Life of Christ in Stereo*. Edited by Stanley A. Ellisen. Portland, OR, 1969.

Chwolson, D. *Das letzte Passamahl Christi und der Tages seines Todes*. 2nd ed. Leipzig, 1908.

Conzelmann, Hans. *History of Primitive Christianity*. Translated by John E. Steely. Nashville, 1973.

Creed, John Martin. *The Gospel according to St. Luke*. London, 1930.

Crook, John. *Concilium Principis*. Cambridge, 1955.

Cullmann, Oscar. *The Early Church*. Edited by A. J. B. Higgins. Philadelphia, 1956.

Dalman, Gustaf. *Arbeit und Sitte in Palästina*. 7 vols. Güttersloh, 1928-42.

_____. *Jesus-Jeshua*. Translated by Paul P. Levertoff. London, 1929.

Dancy, J. C. *A Commentary on I Maccabees*. Oxford, 1954.

Deissmann, Adolf. *Light from the Ancient East*. Translated by Lionel R. M. Strachen. 4th ed. New York, 1927.

Dibelius, Martin. *From Tradition to Gospel*. Translated by Bertram Lee Woolf. 2nd ed. London, 1934.

Dodd, C. H. *Historical Tradition in the Fourth Gospel*. Cambridge, 1963.

_____. *Interpretation of the Fourth Gospel*. Cambridge, 1954.

_____. *Parables of the Kingdom*. 3rd ed. London, 1936.

Dupraz, L. *De l'association de Tibère au principat à la naissance du Christ*. Vol. XLIII of *Studia Friburgensia*. Fribourg, 1966.

Edersheim, Alfred. *The Life and Times of Jesus the Messiah*. 2 vols. 3rd ed. London, 1886.

Eisler, Robert. ΙΗΣΟΥΣ ΒΑΣΙΛΕΥΣ ΟΥ ΒΑΣΙΛΕΥΣΑΣ. 2 vols. Heidelberg, 1929.

_____. *The Messiah Jesus and John the Baptist*. Translated Alexander Haggerty Krappe. New York, 1931.

Ellicott, C. J. *Historical Lectures on the Life of Our Lord Jesus Christ*. London, 1861.

Field, Frederick. *Notes on Select Passages of the Greek Testament*. Oxford, 1881.

Finegan, Jack. *Handbook of Biblical Chronology*. Princeton, 1964.

Finkel, Asher. *The Pharisees and the Teacher of Nazareth*. London, 1964.

Frank, Edgar. *Talmudic and Rabbinical Chronology*. New York, 1956.

Fuller, Reginald H. *The Mission and Achievement of Jesus*. London, 1954.

Geldenhuys, Norval. *Commentary on the Gospel of Luke*. London, 1950.

Godet, Frederick Louis. *Commentary on the Gospel of John*. Translated by Timothy Dwight. 3rd ed. New York, 1886.

_____. *A Commentary on the Gospel of St Luke*. Translated by

E. W. Shalders and M. D. Cusin. 2 vols. Edinburgh, n.d.

Goguel, Maurice. *The Life of Jesus*. Translated by Olive Wyon. London, 1933.

Goldstine, Herman H. *New and Full Moons, 1001 B.C. to A.D. 1651*. Philadelphia, 1973.

Goodenough, Edwin R. *Jewish Symbols in Greco-Roman Period*. 13 vols. New York, 1953-68.

Goss, Glenn Richard. "The Chronological Problems of the Seventy Weeks of Daniel." Unpublished Th.D. dissertation, Dallas Theological Seminary, 1966.

Goudoever, J. van. *Biblical Calendars*. 2nd ed. Leiden, 1961.

Guigneburt, Ch. *Jesus*. Translated by S. H. Hooke. London, 1935.

Gundry, Robert H. *The Church and the Tribulation*. Grand Rapids, 1973.

Guthrie, Donald. *New Testament Introduction*. 3rd ed. Downers Grove, IL, 1970.

Hendriksen, William. *Exposition of the Gospel according to John*. 2 vols. Grand Rapids, 1953-54.

_____. *Exposition of the Gospel according to Matthew*. Grand Rapids, 1973.

Hengstenberg, E. W. *Christology of the Old Testament*. Translated by Theodore Meyer and James Martin. 4 vols. Edinburgh, 1872-78.

Higgins, A. J. B. *The Lord's Supper in the New Testament*. London, 1952.

Hoehner, Harold W. "Chronology of the Apostolic Age." Unpublished Th.D. dissertation, Dallas Theological Seminary, 1965.

_____. *Herod Antipas*. Cambridge, 1972.

Holtzman, Fred. "A Re-examination of the Seventy Weeks of Daniel." Unpublished Th.M. thesis, Dallas Theological Seminary, 1974.

Instinsky, Hans Ulrich. *Das Jahr der Geburt Christi*. München, 1957.

James, E. O. *Seasonal Feasts and Festivals*. New York, 1961.

Jastrow, Marcus, comp. *A Dictionary of the Targumim, the Talmud Bibli Yerushalmi, and the Midrashic Literature*. 2 vols. London, 1903.

Jaubert, Annie. *The Date of the Last Supper*. Translated by Isaac Rafferty. New York, 1965.

Jeremias, Joachim. *The Eucharistic Words of Jesus*. Translated by Norman Perrin. 3rd ed. London, 1966.

_____. *Jerusalem in the Time of Jesus.* Translated from the 3rd German edition (1962) and revised in 1967 by F. H. and C. H. Cave. Philadelphia, 1969.

Keil, C. F. *Biblical Commentary on the Book of Daniel.* Translated by M. G. Easton. Edinburgh, 1876.

_____. *The Books of Ezra, Nehemiah, and Esther.* Translated by Sophia Taylor. Edinburgh, 1873.

Keim, Theodor. *The History of Jesus of Nazareth.* Translated by E. M. Geldart and Arthur Ransom. 6 vols. London, 1873-83.

Klausner, Joseph. *Jesus of Nazareth.* Translated by Herbert Danby. London, 1925.

Koehler, Ludwig and Baumgartner, Walter, eds. *Lexicon in Veteris Testamenti Libros.* Leiden, 1958.

Kümmel, Werner Georg. *Introduction to the New Testament.* Translated by Howard Clark Kee. 17th revised ed. Nashville, 1975.

Lagrange, M.-J. *The Gospel of Jesus Christ.* Translated by the Members of the English Dominican Province. London, 1938.

Lane, William L. *The Gospel according to Mark.* Grand Rapids, 1974.

Leupold, H. C. *Exposition of Daniel.* Columbus, OH, 1949.

Levick, Barbara. *Roman Colonies in Southern Asia Minor.* Oxford, 1967.

Lewin, Thomas. *Fasti Sacri or a Key to the Chronology of the New Testament.* London, 1865.

Liddell, Henry George and Scott, Robert, comps. *A Greek-English Lexicon.* New edition revised and augmented by Henry Stuart Jones. 9th ed. Oxford, 1940.

Lietzmann, Hans. *Mass and Lord's Supper.* Translated by Dorothea H. G. Reeve. London, 1953-54.

Lindars, Barnabas. *The Gospel of John.* London, 1972.

Loisy, Alfred. *Les Évangiles Synoptiques.* 2 vols. Paris, 1907-8.

M'Neile, Alan Hugh. *The Gospel according to St. Matthew.* London, 1915.

Madden, Frederic W. *Coins of the Jews.* Vol. II of *The International Numismata Orientalia.* London, 1881.

Madison, Leslie P. "Problems of Chronology in the Life of Christ." Unpublished Th.D dissertation, Dallas Theological Seminary, 1963.

Manson, T. W. *The Sayings of Jesus.* London, 1949.

Marsh, Frank Burr. *The Reign of Tiberius.* London, 1931.

Meyer, Eduard. *Ursprung and Anfänge des Christentums*. 3 vols. Stuttgart and Berlin, 1921-23.

Mommsen, Theodor. *Römisches Staatsrecht*. 3 vols. 3rd ed. Leipzig, 1887-88.

Montgomery, James A. *A Critical and Exegetical Commentary on the Book of Daniel*. New York, 1927.

Morris, Leon. *The Gospel according to John*. Grand Rapids, 1971.

Moule, C. F. D. *An Idiom Book of New Testament Greek*. 2nd ed. Cambridge, 1959.

Moulton, James Hope. *Prolegomena*. Vol. I of *A Grammar of the New Testament Greek*ᵢ. 3rd ed. Edinburgh, 1908.

Ogg, George. *The Chronology of the Public Ministry of Jesus*. Cambridge, 1940.

———. *The Odyssey of Paul*. Old Tappan, NJ, 1968.

Olmstead, A. T. *Jesus in the Light of History*. New York, 1942.

Parker, Richard A. and Dubberstein, Waldo H. *Babylonian Chronology 626 B.C.—A.D. 75*. 2nd ed. Providence, 1956.

Payne, J. Barton. *Encyclopedia of Biblical Prophecy*. New York, 1973.

———. *The Imminent Appearing of Christ*. Grand Rapids, 1962.

———. *The Theology of the Older Testament*. Grand Rapids, 1962.

Pickl, Josef. *The Messias*. Translated by Andrew Green. St. Louis, 1946.

Plummer, Alfred. *The Gospel according to S. Luke*. 4th ed. Edinburgh, 1905.

Porteous, Norman W. *Daniel: A Commentary*. London, 1965.

Pusey, E. B. *Daniel the Prophet*. Oxford, 1876.

Ramsay, W. M. *The Bearing of Recent Discoveries on the Trustworthiness of the New Testament*. 4th ed. London, 1920.

———. *St. Paul the Traveller and the Roman Citizen*. 14th ed. London, 1920.

———. *Was Christ Born at Bethlehem?* 2nd ed. London, 1898.

Reicke, Bo. *The New Testament Era*. Translated by David E. Green. Philadelphia, 1968.

Robertson, A. T. *A Grammar of the Greek New Testament in the Light of Historical Research*. 4th ed. New York, 1923.

———. *A Harmony of the Gospel for Students of the Life of Christ*. New York, 1922.

Ruckstuhl, Eugen. *Chronology of the Last Days of Jesus*. Translated by Victor J. Drapela. New York, 1965.

151

Schnackenburg, Rudolf. *The Gospel according to St. John.* Translated by Kevin Smyth. New York, 1956.

Schonfield, Hugh J. *The Jesus Party.* New York, 1974.

Schürer, Emil. *A History of the Jewish People in the Age of Jesus.* Revised and edited by Geza Vermes, Fergus Millar, and Matthew Black. Vol. I. Edinburgh, 1973.

Scroggie, W. Graham. *A Guide to the Gospels.* London, 1948.

Segal, J. B. *The Hebrew Passover.* London, 1963.

Sherwin-White, A. N. *Roman Society and Roman Law in the New Testament.* Oxford, 1963.

Slotki, Judah J. *Daniel, Ezra and Nehemiah.* London, 1951.

Smith, David. *The Life and Letters of St. Paul.* London, 1919.

Smith, Dwight Moody, Jr. *The Composition and Order of the Fourth Gospel.* New Haven, 1965.

Stauffer, Ethelbert. *Jerusalem und Rom.* Bern and München, 1957.

———. *Jesus and His Story.* Translated by Dorothea M. Barton. London, 1960.

Strack, Hermann L. and Billerbeck, Paul. *Kommentar zum Neuen Testament aus Talmud und Midrash.* 6 vols. München, 1922-61.

Sutcliffe, Edmond F. *A Two Year Public Ministry Defended.* London, 1938.

Taylor, Vincent. *The Gospel according to St. Mark.* 2nd ed. London, 1966.

Thiele, Edwin R. *The Mysterious Numbers of the Hebrew Kings.* 2nd ed. Grand Rapids, 1965.

Turner, Nigel. *Grammatical Insights into the New Testament.* Edinburgh, 1965.

———. *Syntax.* Vol. III of *A Grammar of New Testament Greek.* Edinburgh, 1963.

Vaux, Roland de. *Ancient Israel: Its Life and Institutions.* Translated by John McHugh. London, 1961.

Velikovsky, Immanuel. *Worlds in Collision.* Garden City, NY, 1950.

Walvoord, John F. *Daniel: The Key to the Prophetic Revelation.* Chicago, 1971.

Wellhausen, J. *Prolegomena zur Geschichte Israels.* 6th ed. Berlin, 1905.

Westcott, B. F. *The Gospel according to St. John.* London, 1882.

———. *An Introduction to the Study of the Gospels.* 6th ed. Cambridge and London, 1881.

Westcott, Brooke Foss and Hort, Fenton John Anthony. *The New Testament in the Original Greek: Introduction, Appendix.* Cambridge and London, 1882.

Whitcomb, John C. Jr. *Darius the Mede.* Grand Rapids, 1959.

Wickes, William. *A Treatise on the Accentuation of the Twenty-one So-called Prose Books of the Old Testament.* Oxford, 1887.

Wieseler, Karl. *Beiträge zur richtigen Würdigung der Evangelien und der evangelischen Geschichte.* Gotha, 1869.

————. *A Chronological Synopsis of the Four Gospels.* Translated by Edmund Venables. 2nd ed. London, 1877.

————. *Chronologische Synopse der vier Evangelium.* Hamburg, 1843.

Wilson, William Riley. *The Execution of Jesus.* New York, 1970.

Winter, Paul. *On the Trial of Jesus.* Vol. I of *Studia Judaica.* Berlin, 1961.

Wood, Leon. *A Commentary on Daniel.* Grand Rapids, 1973.

Young, Edward J. *An Introduction to the Old Testament.* Revised ed. Grand Rapids, 1960.

————. *The Messianic Prophecies of Daniel.* Grand Rapids, 1954.

————. *The Prophecy of Daniel: A Commentary.* Grand Rapids, 1949.

Zahn, Theodor. *Das Evangelium des Lucas.* Leipzig, 1913.

Zeitlin, Solomon. *The Rise and Fall of the Judaean State.* 2 vols. Philadelphia, 1962-67.

Zerwick, Maximilian. *Biblical Greek.* Translated and adapted from the 4th Latin ed. by Joseph Smith. Rome, 1963.

Periodical Articles

Aldrich, J. K. "The Crucifixion on Thursday—Not Friday." *Bibliotheca Sacra* XXVII (July, 1870), 401-29.

Bammel, Ernst. "Φίλος τοῦ Καίσαρος." *Theologische Literaturzeitung* LXXVII (April, 1952), 205-10.

————. "Syrian Coinage and Pilate." *The Journal of Jewish Studies* II (1951), 108-10.

Barnes, Timothy D. "The Date of Herod's Death." *The Journal of Theological Studies* XIX (April, 1968), 204-9.

Barrett, C. K. "Luke XXII.15: To Eat the Passover." *The*

Journal of Theological Studies IX (April, 1958), 305-7.

Beckwith, Roger T. "The Day, its Divisions and its Limits, in Biblical Thought." *The Evangelical Quarterly* XLIII (October–December, 1971), 218-27.

Belser, Johannes. "Zur Hypothese von der einjährigen Wirksamkeit Jesu." *Biblische Zeitschrift* I (1903), 55-63, 160-74.

_____. "Zu der Perikope von der Speisung der Fünftausend." *Biblische Zeitschrift* II (1904), 154-76.

Blinzler, Josef. "Eine Bemerkung zum Geschichtsrahmen des Johannesevangeliums." *Biblica* XXXVI (1955), 20-35.

_____. "Die Niedermetzelung von Galiläern durch Pilatus." *Novum Testamentum* II (January, 1957), 24-29.

_____. "Qumran-Kalendar und Passionchronologie." *Zeitschrift für die neutestamentliche Wissenschaft* XLIX (1958), 238-51.

Box, G. H. "The Jewish Antecedents of the Eucharist." *The Journal of Theological Studies* III (April, 1902), 357-69.

Braunert, Horst. "Der römische Provinzialzensus und der Schätungsbericht des Lukas-Evangeliums." *Historia* VI (1957), 192-214.

Christie, W. M. "Did Christ Eat the Passover with His Disciples?" *The Expository Times* XLIII (August, 1932), 515-19.

Cichorius, Conrad. "Chronologisches zum Leben Jesu." *Zeitschrift für die neutestamentliche Wissenschaft* XXII (Juni, 1923), 16-20.

Conybeare, F. C. "The History of Christmas." *The American Journal of Theology* III (January, 1899), 1-21.

Corbishley, Thomas. "The Chronology of the Reign of Herod the Great." *The Journal of Theological Studies* XXXVI (January, 1935), 22-32.

Derrett, J. Duncan M. "Further Light on the Narratives of the Nativity." *Novum Testamentum* XVII (April, 1975), 81-108.

Dieckmann, Hermann. "Die effektive Mitregenschaft des Tiberius." *Klio* XV (1918), 339-75.

Doyle, A. D. "Pilate's Career and the Date of the Crucifixion." *The Journal of Theological Studies* XLII (October, 1941), 190-93.

Driver, G. R. "Two Problems in the New Testament." *The Journal of Theological Studies* XVI (October, 1965), 327-37.

Filmer, W. E. "The Chronology of the Reign of Herod the Great." *The Journal of Theological Studies* XVII (October, 1966), 283-98.

Fotheringham, J. K. "Astronomical Evidence for the Date of the Crucifixion." *The Journal of Theological Studies* XII (October, 1910), 120-27.

_____. "The Evidence of Astronomy and Technical Chronology for the Date of the Crucifixion." *The Journal of Theological Studies* XXXV (April, 1934), 142-62.

Frederick, William. "Did Jesus Eat the Passover?" *Bibliotheca Sacra* LXVIII (July, 1911), 503-9.

Frey, J.-B. "La question des images chez les Juifs. A la lumière des récentes déscourvertes." *Biblica* XV, Fasc. 2 and 3 (1934), 265-300.

Grant, Robert M. "The Occasion of Luke III:1-2." *The Harvard Theological Review* XXXIII (April, 1940), 151-54.

Gruenthaner, Michael J. "The Seventy Weeks." *Catholic Biblical Quarterly* I (January, 1939), 44-54.

Haxles, David J. "The Roman Census & Jesus' Birth. Was Luke Correct?" *Buried History* IX (December, 1973), 113-32; X (March, 1974), 17-31.

Heawood, P. J. "The Beginning of the Jewish Day." *The Jewish Quarterly Review* XXXVI (April, 1945), 393-401.

Hedley, P. L. "Pilate's Arrival in Judaea." *The Journal of Theological Studies* XXXV (January, 1934), 56-58.

Higgins, A. J. B. "The Origin of the Eucharist." *New Testament Studies* I (April, 1955), 200-209.

_____. "Sidelights on Christian Beginnings in the Graeco-Roman World." *The Evangelical Quarterly* XLI (October, 1969), 197-206.

Horn, S. H. and Wood, L. H. "The Fifth-Century Jewish Calendar at Elephantine." *Journal of Near Eastern Studies* XIII (January, 1954), 1-20.

Jackson, J. Lamar. "Christmas." *Review and Expositor* XLI (October, 1944), 388-96.

King, Charles. "The Outlines of New Testament Chronology." *Catholic Biblical Quarterly* CCLXXVIII (January–March, 1945), 129-53.

Kraeling, Carl H. "The Episode of the Roman Standards at Jerusalem." *The Harvard Theological Review* XXXV (October, 1942), 263-89.

_____. "Olmstead's Chronology of the Life of Jesus." *Anglican Theological Review* XXIV (October, 1942), 334-54.

Lagrange, M.-J. "Où en est la question du recensement de Quirinius?" *Revue Biblique* VIII (Janvier, 1911), 60-84.

Lake, Kirsopp. "The Date of Herod's Marriage with Herodias, and the Chronology of the Gospels." *The Expositor,* 8th series, IV (November, 1912), 462-77.

Maier, Paul L. "The Episode of the Golden Roman Shields at Jerusalem." *The Harvard Theological Review* LXII (January, 1969), 109-21.

————. "Sejanus, Pilate, and the Date of the Crucifixion." *Church History* XXXVII (March, 1968), 3-13.

Marsh, Frank Burr. "Roman Parties in the Reign of Tiberius." *The American Historical Review* XXXI (January, 1926), 233-50.

Morgenstern, Julian. "The Calendar of the Book of Jubilees, its Origin and its Character." *Vetus Testamentum* V (January, 1955), 34-76.

————. "Supplementary Studies in the Calendars of Ancient Israel." *The Hebrew Union College Annual* X (1935), 1-148.

Newman, Robert C. "Daniel's Seventy Weeks and the Old Testament Sabbath-Year Cycle." *Journal of the Evangelical Theological Society* XVI (Fall, 1973), 229-34.

Niese, Benedictus. "Zur Chronologie des Josephus." *Hermes* XXVIII, Heft 2 (1893), 194-229.

Ogg, George. "The Quirinius Question Today." *The Expository Times* LXXIX (May, 1968), 231-36.

————. "Review of Mlle Jaubert, *La date de la Cène.*" *Novum Testamentum* III (January, 1959), 149-60.

Olmstead, A. T. "The Chronology of Jesus' Life." *Anglican Theological Review* XXIV (January, 1942), 1-26.

Ozanne, C. G. "Three Textual Problems in Daniel." *The Journal of Theological Studies* XVI (October, 1965), 445-48.

Power, E. "John 2:20 and the Date of the Crucifixion." *Biblica* IX (July, 1928), 257-88.

Reider, Joseph. "Etymological Studies in Biblical Hebrew." *Vetus Testamentum* II (April, 1952), 113-30.

Robinson, E. "The Alleged Discrepancy between John and the Other Evangelists respecting Our Lord's Last Passover." *Bibliotheca Sacra* II (August, 1845), 406-36.

Roos, A. G. "Die Quirinius-Inschrift." *Mnemosyne* IV (1941), 306-18.

Rusk, Roger. "The Day He Died." *Christianity Today.* March 29, 1974, pp. 4-6.

Schwartz, E. "Noch einmal der Tod der Söhne Zebedaei." *Zeitschrift für die neutestamentliche Wissenschaft* XI (Mai, 1910), 89-104.

Shepherd, Massey, Jr. "Are both the Synoptics and John Correct about the Date of Jesus' Death?" *Journal of Biblical Literature* LXXX (March, 1961), 123-32.

Smallwood, E. Mary. "The Date of the Dismissal of Pontius Pilate from Judaea." *The Journal of Jewish Studies* V, No. 1 (1954), 12-21.

———. "Some Notes on the Jews under Tiberius." *Latomus* XV (Juillet–Septembre, 1956), 314-29.

Stauffer, Ethelbert. "Zur Münzprägung und Judenpolitik des Pontius Pilatus." *La Nouvelle Clio* I/II (October, 1950), 495-514.

Stroes, H. R. "Does the Day Begin in the Evening or Morning?" *Vetus Testamentum* XVI (October, 1966), 460-75.

Syme, Ronald. "Galatia and Pamphylia under Augustus: The Governorships of Piso, Quirinius, and Silvanus." *Klio* XXVII (1934), 122-48.

Taylor, Lily Ross. "Quirinius and the Census of Judaea." *The American Journal of Philology* LIV (April, May, June, 1933), 120-33.

Teeple, Howard M. "Methodology in Source Analysis of the Fourth Gospel." *Journal of Biblical Literature* LXXXI (September, 1962), 279-86.

Torrey, Charles C. "The Date of the Crucifixion according to the Fourth Gospel." *Journal of Biblical Literature* L (December, 1931), 227-41.

———. "In the Fourth Gospel the Last Supper was the Paschal Meal." *The Jewish Quarterly Review* XLII (January, 1952), 237-50.

Walker, Norman. "Pauses in the Passion Story and their Significance for Chronology." *Novum Testamentum* VI (January, 1963), 16-19.

Windisch, Hans. "Die Dauer der öffentlichen Wirksamkeit Jesus nach den vier Evangelisten." *Zeitschrift für die neutestamentliche Wissenschaft* XII (1911), 141-75.

Zeitlin, Solomon. "The Beginning of the Jewish Day during the Second Commonwealth." *The Jewish Quarterly Review* XXXVI (April, 1945), 403-14.

———. "Megillat Taanit as a Source for Jewish Chronology and History in the Hellenistic and Roman Periods." *The Jewish Quarterly Review* X (October, 1919 and January, 1920), 237-90.

Essays

Black, M. "The Arrest and Trial of Jesus and the Date of the Last Supper." *New Testament Essays*. Edited by A. J. B. Higgins. Manchester, 1959, pp. 19-33.

Duncan, George B. "Chronology." *The Interpreter's One-Volume Commentary on the Bible*. Edited by Charles M. Laymon. Nashville, 1971, pp. 1271-82.

Heichelheim, F. M. "Roman Syria." *An Economic Survey of Ancient Rome*. Edited by Tenney Frank. Vol. IV. Baltimore, 1938, pp. 121-257.

Hölscher, Gustav. "Die Hohenpriesterliste bei Josephus und die evangelische Chronologie." *Sitzungsberichte der Heidelberger Akadamie der Wissenschaften — Philosophisch-historische Klasse*. Vol. XXX. Heidelberg, 1940, pp. 1-33.

Kline, Meredith G. "The Covenant of the Seventieth Week." *The Law and Prophets. Old Testament Studies Prepared in Honor of Oswald Thompson Allis*. Edited by John H. Skilton. Nutley, NJ, 1974, pp. 452-69.

Knight, George A. F. "The Book of Daniel." *The Interpreter's One-Volume Commentary on the Bible*. Edited by Charles M. Laymon. Nashville, 1971, pp. 436-50.

Moehring, Horst R. "The Census in Luke as an Apologetic Device." *Studies in the New Testament and Early Christian Literature*. Edited by David Edward Aune. *Supplements to Novum Testamentum*. Vol. XXXIII. Leiden, 1972, pp. 144-60.

Morgenstern, Julian. "The New Year for Kings." *Occident and Orient. Being Studies in Semitic Philology and Literature, Jewish History and Philosophy and Folklore in the Widest Sense in Honour of Haham Dr. M. Gaster's 80th Birthday*. Edited by Bruno Schindler. London, 1936, pp. 439-56.

Ogg, George. "The Chronology of the Last Supper." *Theological Collections VI: Historicity and Chronology in the New Testament*. London, 1965, pp. 75-96.

———. "Chronology of the New Testament." *Peake's Commentary on the Bible*. Edited by Matthew Black. London, 1962, pp. 728-32.

Stevenson, G. H. "The Imperial Administration." *The Cambridge Ancient History*. Edited by S. A. Cook, F. E. Adcock, and M. P. Charlesworth. Vol. X. Cambridge, 1934, pp. 182-217.

Dictionary and Encyclopedia Articles

Abrahams, Israel. "Time." *A Dictionary of the Bible*. Edited by James Hastings, *et al*. IV (1902): 762-66.

Armstrong, William P. "Chronology of the New Testament." *The International Standard Bible Encyclopedia*. Edited by James Orr, *et al*. I (1929): 644-50.

Bickerman, E. J. "Calendar, III. Ancient Middle Eastern Calendar Systems: Lunisolar Calendars in Antiquity." *Encyclopaedia Britannica*. III (15th ed., 1974): 604-5.

_____. "Makkabäerbücher." *Realencyclopädie der klassischen Altertumswissenschaft*. Edited by A. Pauly and Georg Wissowa. XIV, 1 (1928): 779-800.

Bruce, Frederick Fyvie. "Census." *Twentieth Century Encyclopedia of Religious Knowledge*. Edited by Lefferts A. Loetscher. I (1955): 222.

_____. "Quirinius." *The New Bible Dictionary*. Edited by J. D. Douglas. (1962): 1069.

Buitenen, J. A. B. van. "Calendar, IV. The Far East: The Hindu Calendar." *Encyclopaedia Britannica*. III (15th ed., 1974): 606-8.

Caird, George B. "The Chronology of the NT." *The Interpreter's Dictionary of the Bible*. Edited by George Arthur Buttrick, *et al*. I (1962): 599-607.

Drower, Margret Stefana. "Chronology, III. Egyptian." *Encyclopaedia Britannica*. V (14th ed., 1972): 722-24.

Filiozat, Jean Lucien Antoine. "Calendar, V. Hindu Calendar." *Encyclopaedia Britannica*. IV (14th ed., 1972): 621-622.

Helck, Wolfgang. "Chronology: Egyptian." *Encyclopaedia Britannica*. IV (15th ed., 1974): 575-76.

Lake, Kirsopp. "Christmas." *Encyclopedia of Religion and Ethics*. Edited by James Hastings, *et al*. III (1910): 601-8.

Lewy, Hildegard. "Calendar, VI. Babylonian and Assyrian Calendars." *Encyclopaedia Britannica*. IV (14th ed., 1972): 622-23.

McLaughlin, J. F. "New Year." *The Jewish Encyclopedia.* Edited by I. Singer, *et al.* IX (1895): 254-56.

Morgenstern Julian. "New Year." *The Interpreter's Dictionary of the Bible.* Edited by George Arthur Buttrick, *et al.* III (1962): 544-46.

————. "Year." *The Interpreter's Dictionary of the Bible.* Edited by George Arthur Buttrick, *et al.* IV (1962): 923-24.

Ogg, G. "Chronology of the New Testament." *The New Bible Dictionary.* Edited by J. D. Douglas. (1962): 223-28.

Poet, T. Eric. "Calendar, IV. Egyptian Calendar." *Encyclopaedia Britannica.* VI (14th ed., 1972): 620-21.

Proskouriakoff, Tatiana. "Calendar, V. Calendar Systems of the Americas." *Encyclopaedia Britannica.* III (15th ed., 1974): 609-12.

Ramsay, William M. "Numbers, Hours, Years, and Dates." *A Dictionary of the Bible.* Edited by James Hastings, *et al.* Extra Volume (1904): 473-84.

Robson, John Adam. "Chronology, VIII. Christian." *Encyclopaedia Britannica.* V (14th ed., 1972): 728.

Schmidt, John D. "Calendar, III. Ancient Middle Eastern Calendar Systems: The Egyptian Calendar." *Encyclopaedia Britannica.* III (15th ed., 1974): 606.

Soden, Hermann von. "Chronology. *Encyclopaedia Biblica.* Edited by T. K. Cheyne and T. Sutherland Black. I (1899): 799-819.

Thompson, J. Eric S. "Chronology: Pre-Columbian American." *Encyclopaedia Britannica.* IV (15th ed., 1974): 581-82.

Turner, Cuthbert Hamilton. "Chronology of the New Testament." *A Dictionary of the Bible.* Edited by James Hastings, *et al.* I (1898): 403-25.

Index of Authors

Index of Names and Subjects

Index of Passages Cited

BIBLICAL SOURCES

Old Testament

APOCRYPHAL LITERATURE

RABBINIC SOURCES

The Mishnah

The Babylonian Talmud

EARLY CHRISTIAN SOURCES